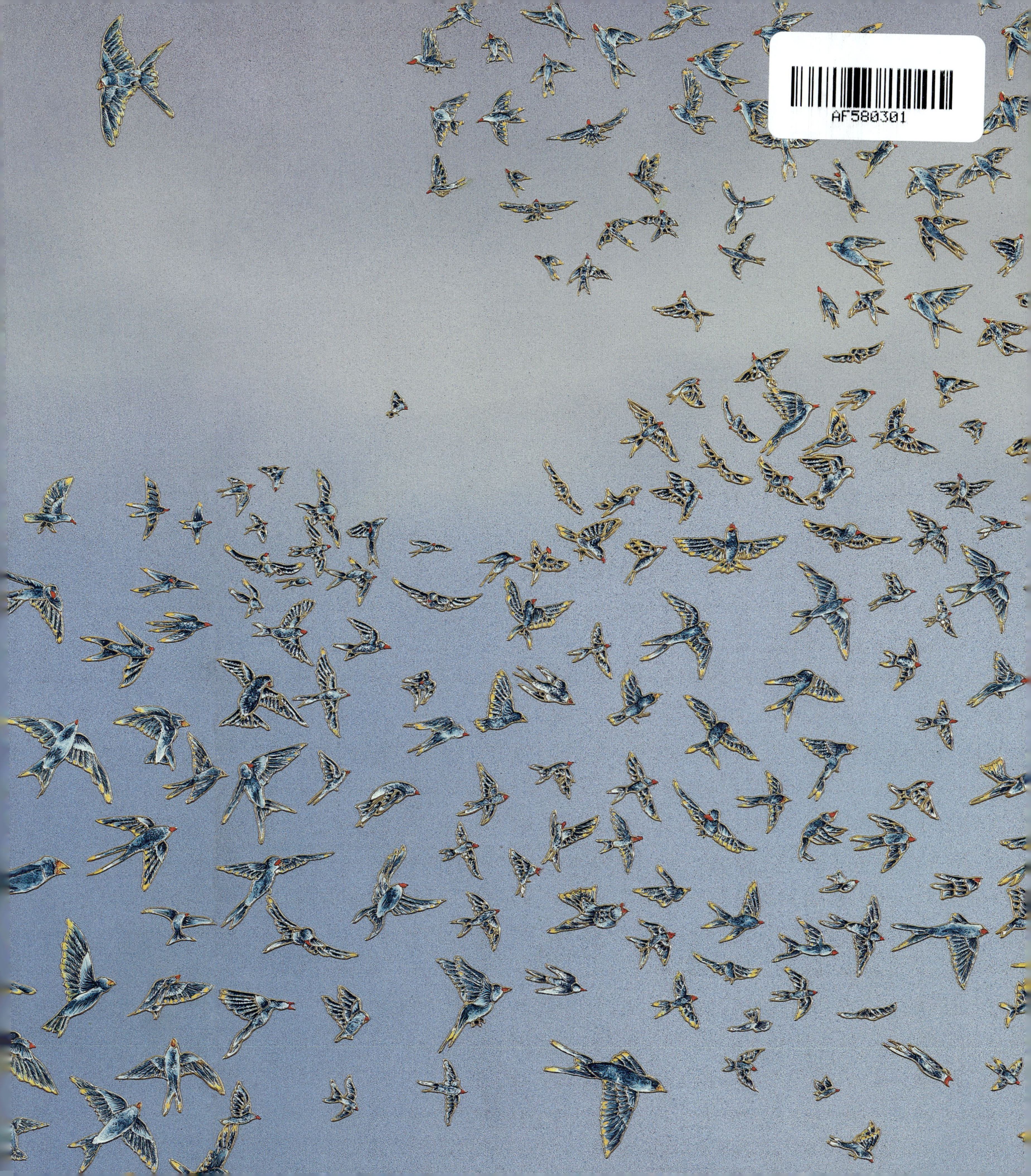

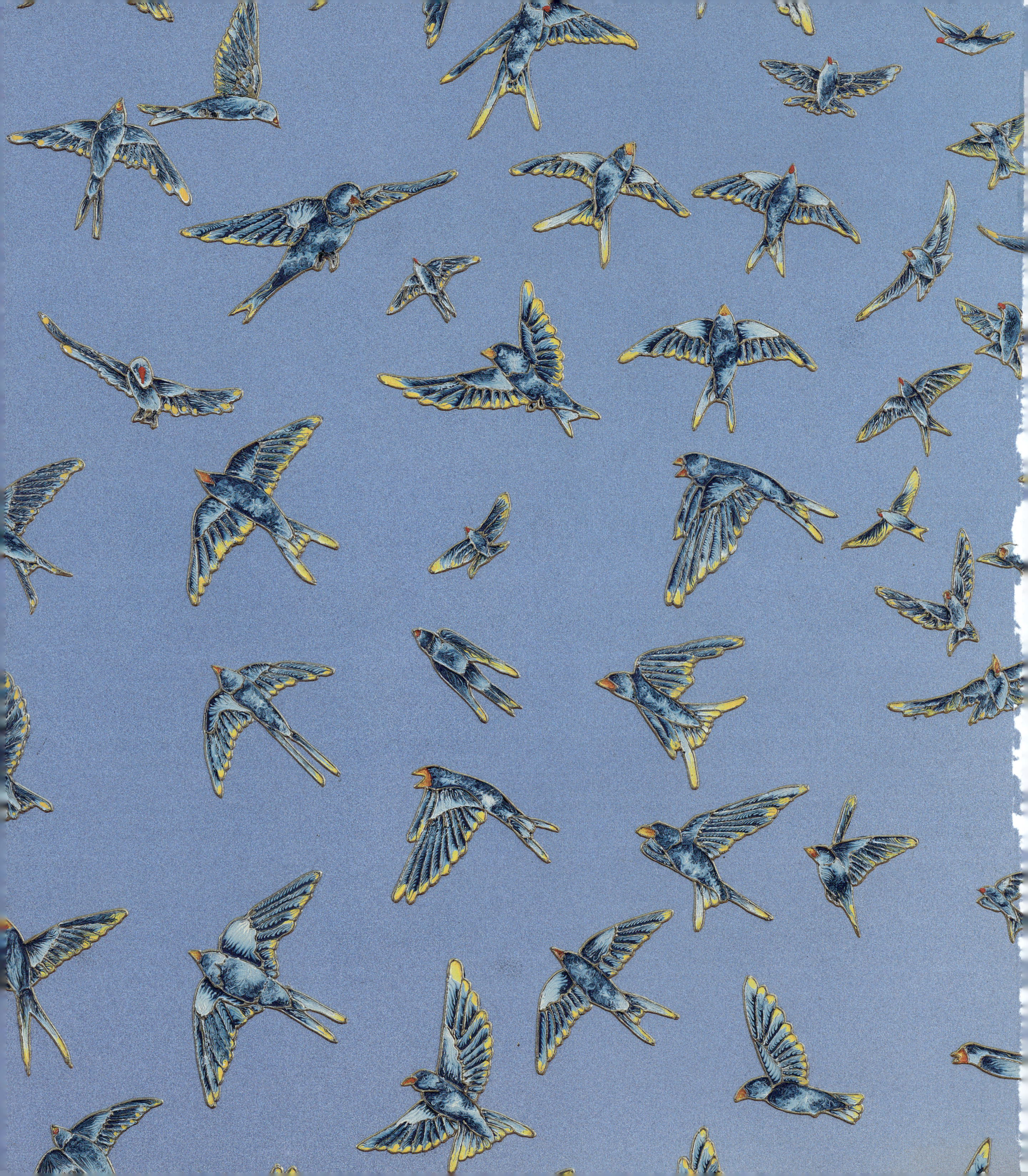

Raqib Shaw

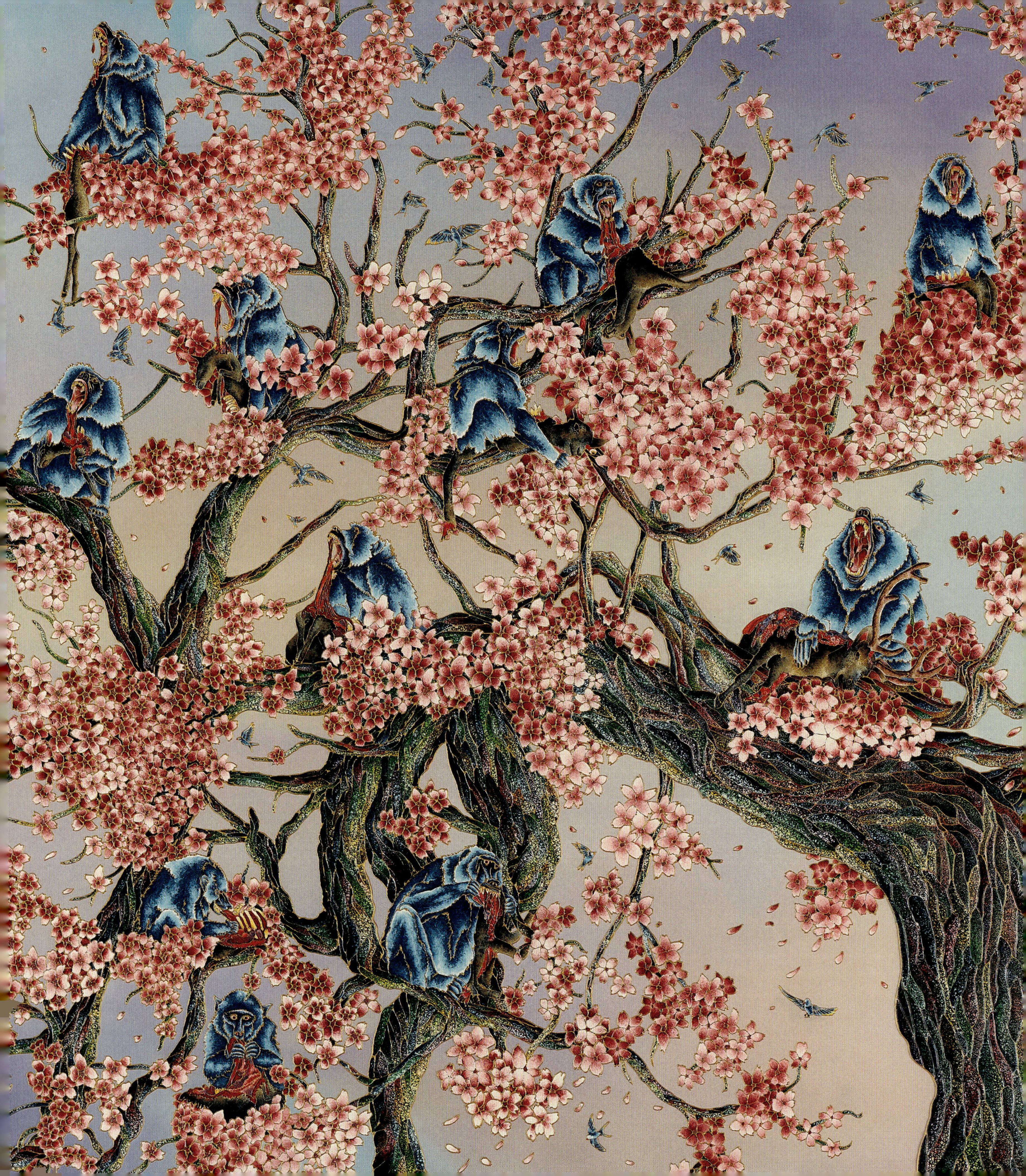

Raqib Shaw

Paradise Lost

EDITED BY
James Rondeau

ESSAYS BY
Madhuvanti Ghose
and David Lomas

The Art Institute of Chicago

Distributed by Yale University Press,
New Haven and London

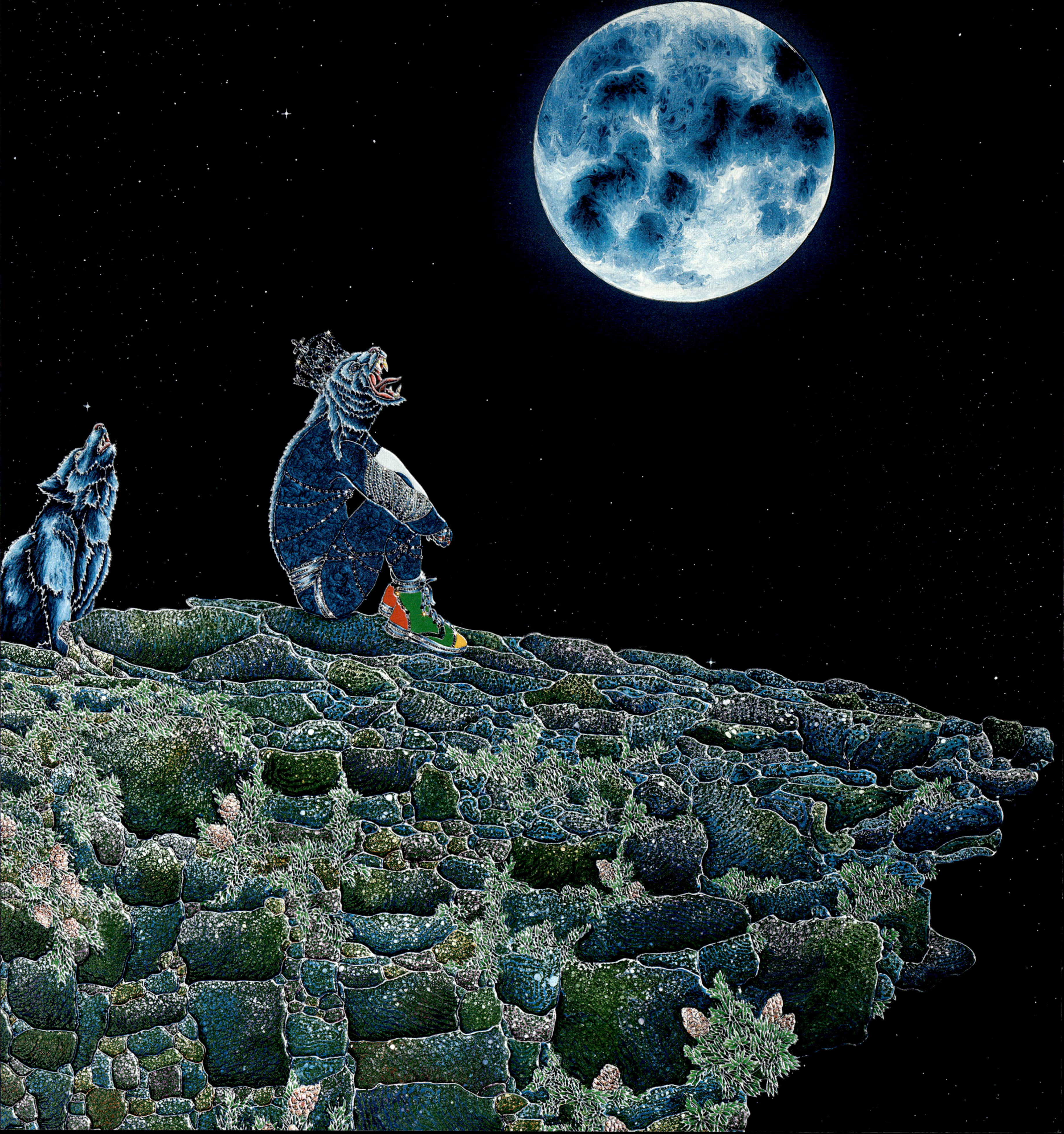

Contents

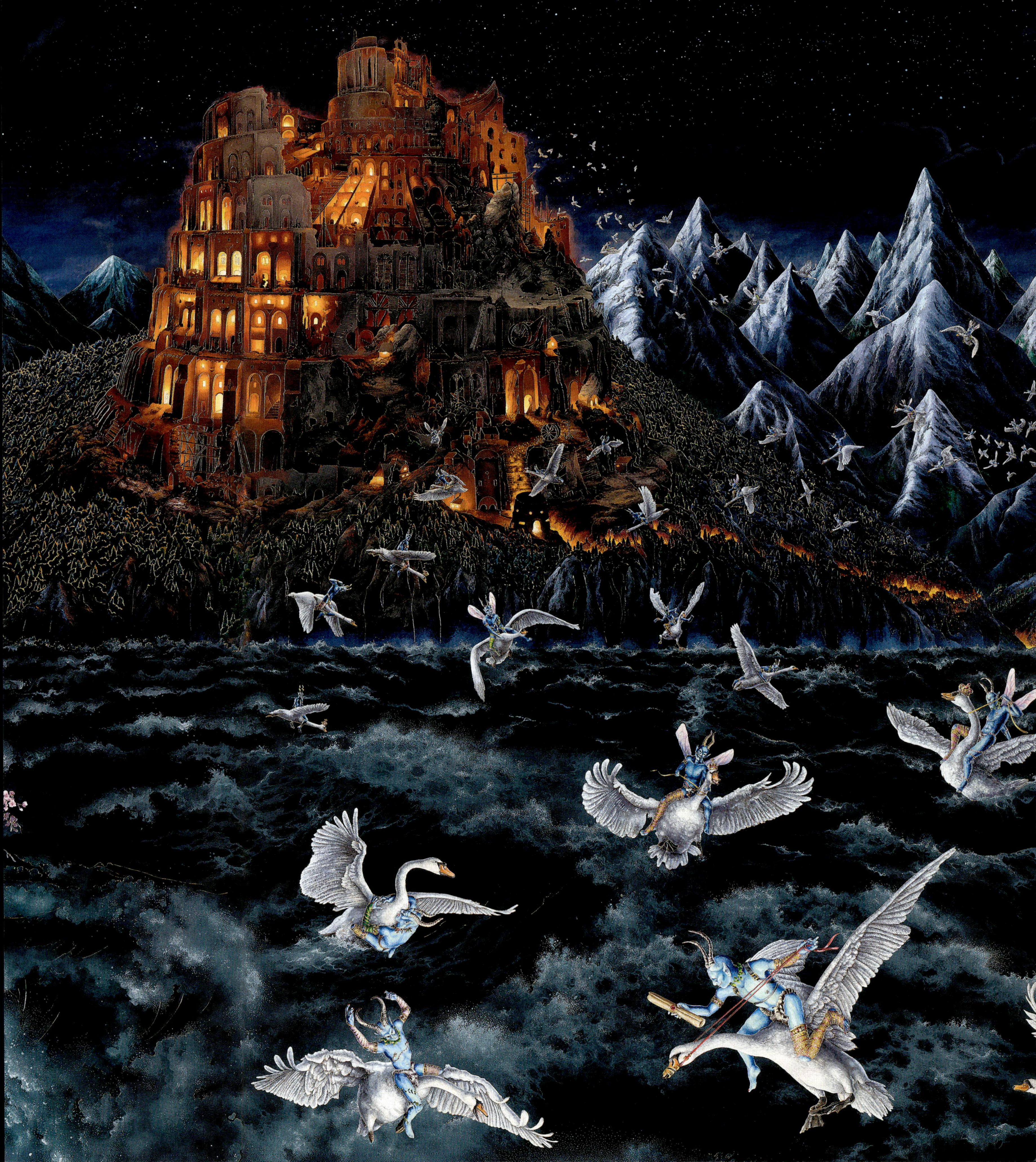

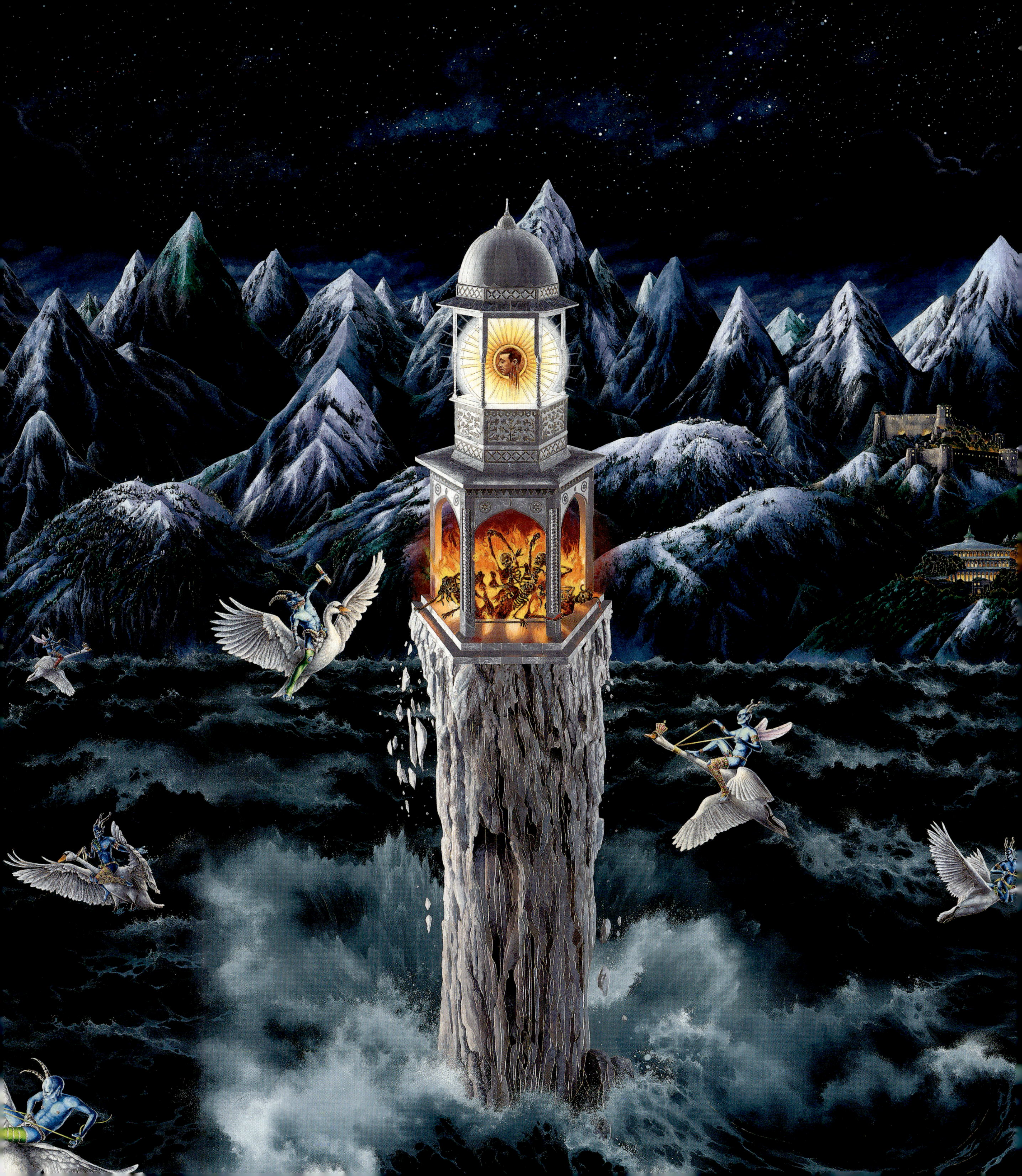

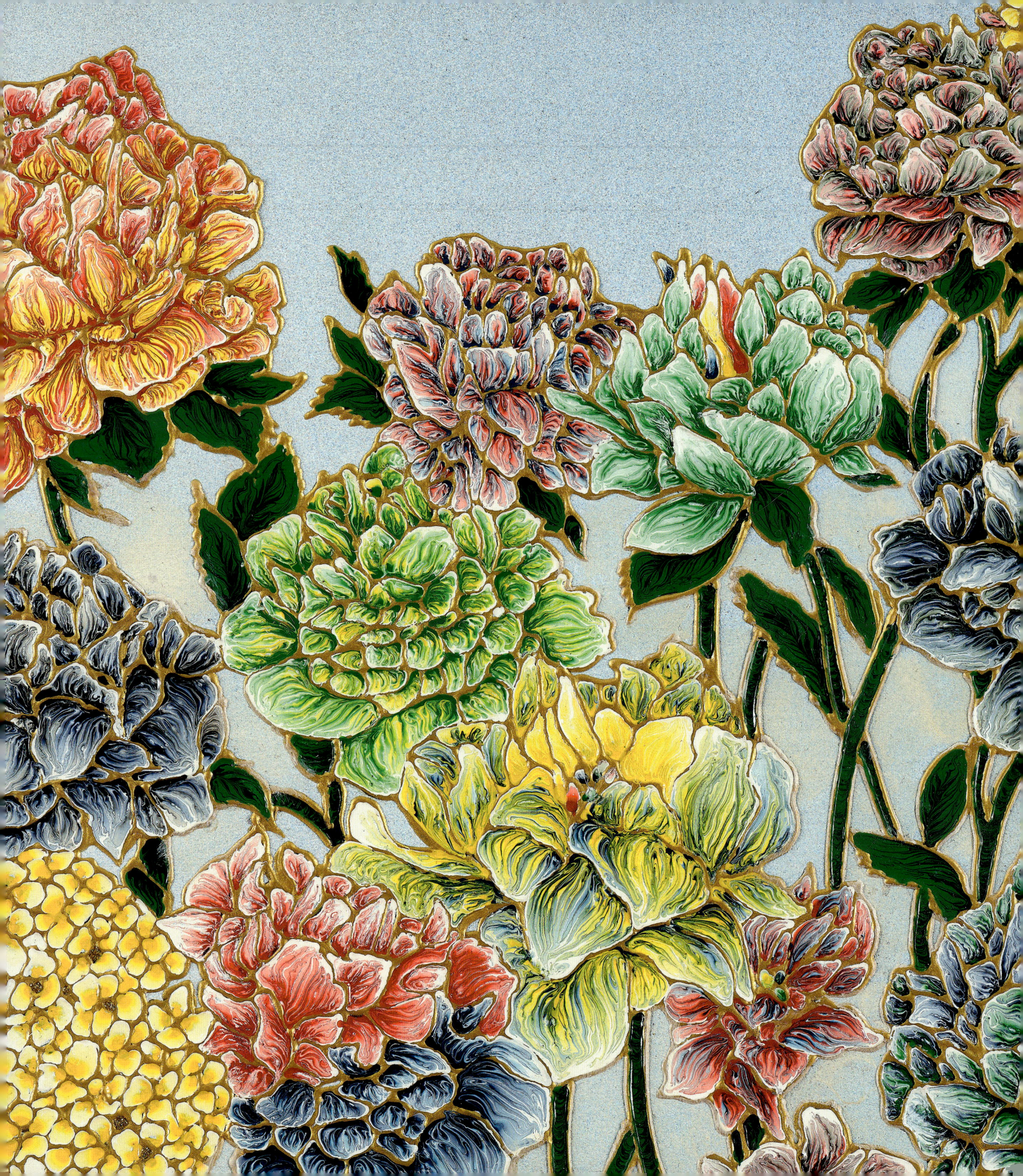

I have had the pleasure and privilege of seeing Raqib Shaw's monumental painting *Paradise Lost* at various stages of its creation, spanning more than a decade. From the earliest panels in his studio to the extraordinary completed work, I have watched Raqib's emotional journey as an artist unfold.

This presentation at the Art Institute of Chicago is the premiere of a newly completed section of *Paradise Lost*, and I am thrilled that the museum's visitors have the first opportunity to experience its thought-provoking opulence and intricacy.

The exhibition and this accompanying publication celebrate Raqib's signature accomplishment. It has been a great honor to support the presentation and to ensure that Raqib's powerful work reaches new audiences across the globe.

USHA MITTAL
Trustee
The Art Institute of Chicago

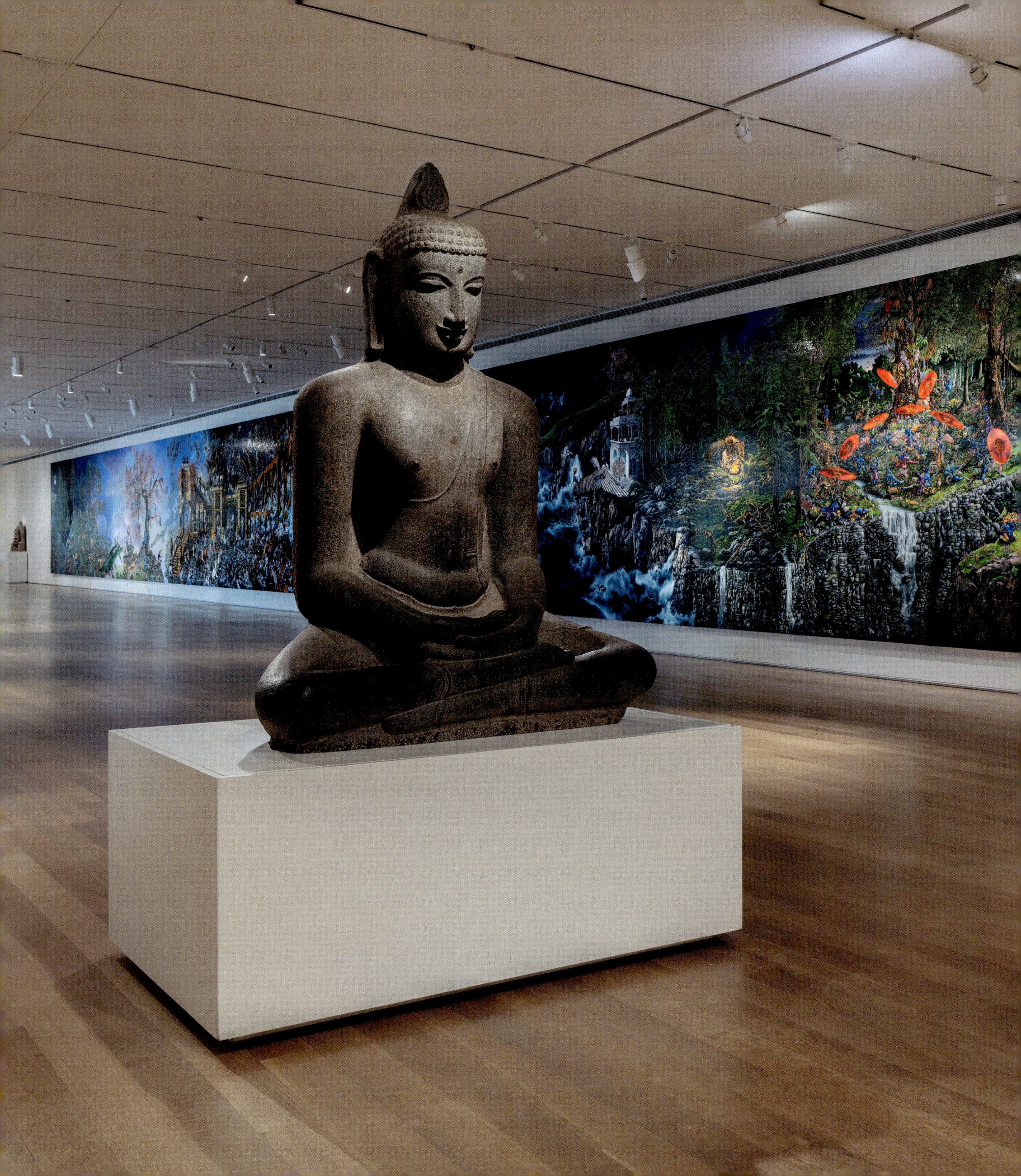

Foreword and Introduction

Raqib Shaw's epic multipart painting *Paradise Lost* traverses autobiographical and symbolic narratives in sparkling color and intricate detail. We at the Art Institute of Chicago are honored to debut this herculean effort—more than one hundred feet long and more than twenty years in the making—and share it with our city and the world. This exhibition also marks the first time all four "chapters," or narrative sections, have been displayed together, showcasing this monumental work to its fullest extent yet. Shaw originally conceived of *Paradise Lost* in 1999 and began painting it in 2009; he exhibited the first chapter in 2011. He put down his porcupine quills and pots of enamel in May 2025 to prepare it for shipment to Chicago, but he has said he will be working on the painting for the rest of his life.

Shaw was born in Calcutta, India, in 1974 and raised in the verdant Himalayan mountains of Kashmir. At the age of sixteen, his family moved to New Delhi, fleeing violence in the Kashmir Valley. At eighteen, Shaw left for England alone, where he attended Central Saint Martins; he has lived and worked in London ever since. Shaw's paintings draw on the landscapes and memories of his early life in India and on a broad array of other influences: Mughal and Persian miniatures; Renaissance altarpieces; Japanese art; Kashmiri and Urdu poetry; Hindu and Western mythology; and paintings by the likes of Lucas Cranach the Elder, Gerrit van Honthorst, and Édouard Manet. Despite these diverse inspirations, Shaw's vision, process, and technique are unmistakably his own.

In fact, one struggles to place Shaw's practice in the context of global contemporary painting. *Paradise Lost* is unique and impossible to read through the lens of any one time or place; rather, it demonstrates Shaw's unbridled and unmatched capacity for world-building. Each narrative cycle unfolds almost like a state of cathartic, lucid dreaming. The themes of expulsion and return, damnation and salvation play out across each chapter. While his imagery is often self-referential and tethered to the lived reality of exile from his homeland, Shaw creates a new universe to exist within. This universe is filled with phantasmagoric, otherworldly, and hybrid creatures, landscapes, and architecture—all depicted with razor-sharp clarity. Distinct from the work of his contemporaries, Shaw's visions align more closely to the narrative wall paintings of fourteenth-century Italian artist Giotto or the fantastical works of sixteenth-century Dutch painter Hieronymus Bosch, especially Bosch's enigmatic triptych *The Garden of Earthly Delights* (1490–1500; Museo del Prado), which Shaw directly references in his series of the same title (2003–5). Similar to these early masters, Shaw engages with storytelling through complex symbolic systems—personal, religious, cosmological, mythological, historical, literary—imbuing each element with universal themes of suffering, joy, chaos, peace, love, and loss. It was a privilege to follow the most recent chapter of *Paradise Lost* as it came into fruition. I am grateful to Art Institute Trustee Usha Mittal for bringing us together. Witnessing Shaw at work—both in his studio and in the gardens he has painstakingly cultivated—gave me an acute appreciation for the layers of inspiration that surround him and permeate his art.

We are humbled that Shaw entrusted us with exhibiting this pivotal work, and I would like to thank him for being such an inspiring partner throughout this collaboration. We are also profoundly grateful to

Usha and Lakshmi Niwas Mittal for their unwavering leadership at the museum; their generous support made it possible to bring *Paradise Lost* to Chicago and celebrate it with this publication. I am also thankful to my colleague Madhuvanti Ghose, Alsdorf Associate Curator of Indian, Southeast Asian, and Himalayan Art, for shepherding this project and for expertly reinstalling the Alsdorf Galleries to showcase this piece. Without a doubt, *Paradise Lost* is one of the largest works of art we have ever displayed in our over 150-year history, and it completely transforms the expansive space of Gunsaulus Hall. The Art Institute, with a collection that stretches across time and geographies, allows visitors to experience the present tense of Shaw's cycle in dialogue with the ancient past. Sculptures from the Indian subcontinent have been installed alongside *Paradise Lost* to help contextualize the work in its cultural milieu (see "About the Installation" in this volume).

Epic and intricate, monumental and meticulous—*Paradise Lost* offers a fantastical meditation on identity, transformation, and the redemptive power of beauty. Since the installation of *Paradise Lost*, I have been struck by the magnetic pull this painting has on our visitors, inspiring all who encounter it to reflect on the many paradises lost across a lifetime: childhood innocence, creative freedom, mental tranquility, and cultural belonging. As Shaw has said, "This is not just my story. It is the story of each of us, and the story of our times."

JAMES RONDEAU

President and Eloise W. Martin Director
The Art Institute of Chicago

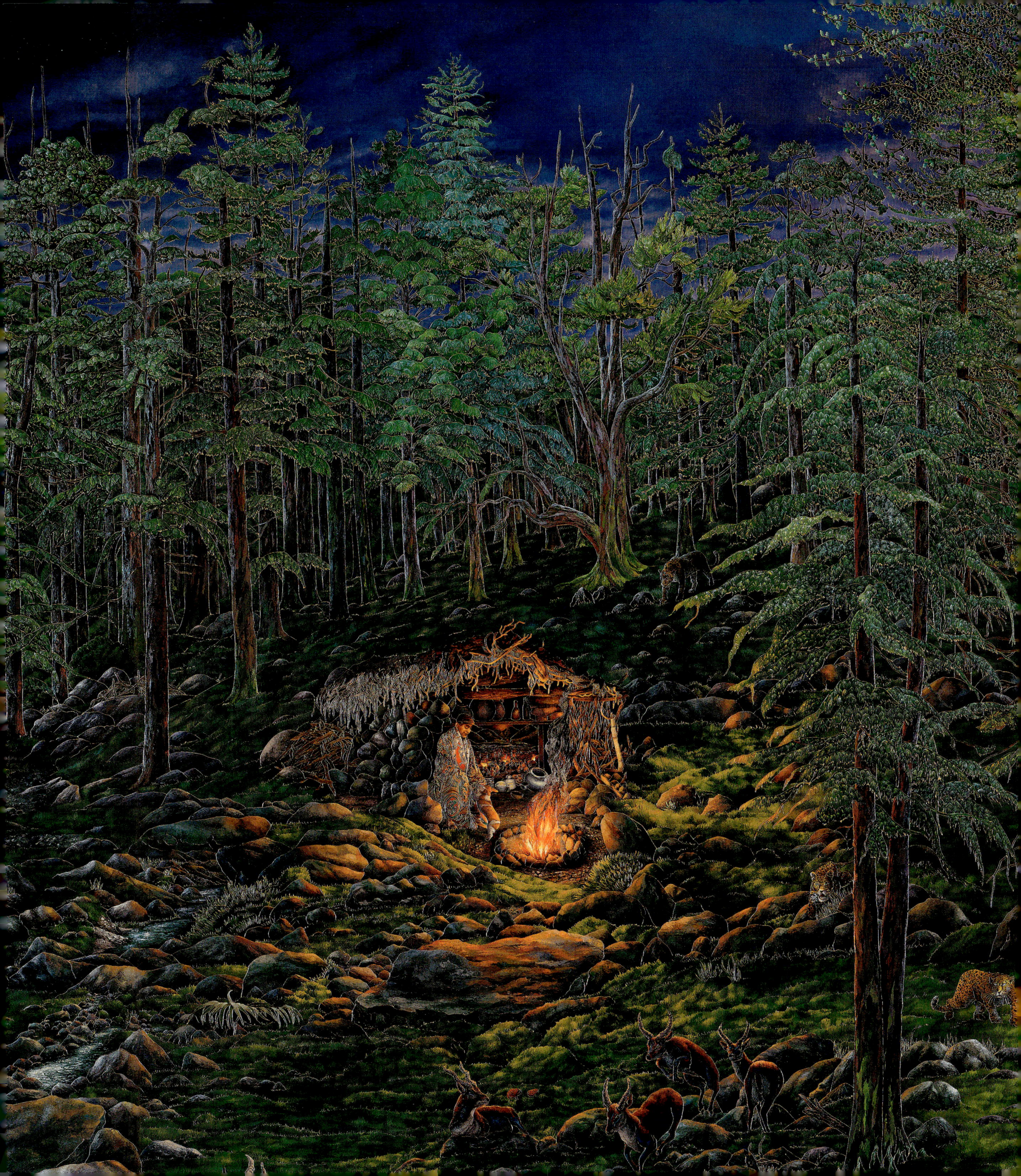

Acknowledgments

There are many people who worked tirelessly to make *Paradise Lost*, both the exhibition and this publication, a success. I am grateful to Raqib Shaw for opening his studio to us and sharing so much of himself in the process. Museum trustee Usha Mittal suggested that we show *Paradise Lost* at the Art Institute, and we are all immensely thankful to her and to her husband, Lakshmi Niwas Mittal, for their extraordinary support throughout.

Shaw's studio and the entire team at Minty Project Management in London were instrumental at every step; Jamie Freeth aided us throughout, including during the installation. Shaw's galleries, particularly Daniela Gareh and Irene Bradbury at White Cube and Arne Glimcher at Pace, enabled this project. Honey Luard brainstormed about this catalogue with me. David Lomas authored an insightful essay in this volume.

At the Art Institute, I thank James Rondeau, President and Eloise W. Martin Director, for leading the extraordinary endeavor to mount this one-hundred-foot-long artwork in our galleries and for trusting me to follow through on his vision. This exhibition and publication have benefited from the enthusiastic guidance of Sarah Guernsey, Deputy Director and Senior Vice President for Curatorial Affairs, who steered this project deftly from its outset. Equally vital has been the leadership of Sarah Kelly Oehler, Field-McCormick Chair and Curator, Arts of the Americas, and Vice President of Curatorial Strategy; David Nacol, Senior Vice President, Philanthropy; Katie Rahn, Senior Vice President, Marketing and Communications; Emily Benedict, Vice President, Campus Operations; Amy Allen, Vice President, Engagement; and Aaron Andersen, Associate Vice President, Financial Planning and Analysis.

The Publishing department, led by Katie Reilly, brought this beautiful publication to fruition. Elizabeth Upenieks, with Lauren Makholm and Isella Sandoval, handled the production. Kati Woock, with guidance from Lisa Meyerowitz, jumped into the project with enormous enthusiasm as soon as she joined the museum, and I am grateful for her skillful editing. Kristie Kahns secured the images and their reproduction rights. Prudence Cuming in London provided stunning photography of the work. In the museum's Imaging department, led by Bonnie Rosenberg, photographers Nathan Keay, Robert Lifson, Jonathan Mathias, Juan Molina Hernandez, and Joe Tallarico captured additional details and installation views, with production support from Elyse Allen, Kaitlyn Fultz Campion, and Hayley Hinsberger. Julia Ma and Miko McGinty at Miko McGinty Inc. created the stunning design for this publication, which invites readers to more closely examine the sparkling details of Shaw's painting. The staff of the Ryerson and Burnham Libraries, particularly Anthony Morgano and Abigail Adams, were crucial research partners.

It would have been impossible to realize this exhibition without the deft project management skills of Kylie Escudero, guided by Becca Schlossberg with Kendall McElhaney. Anna Martín advised on lighting. In Collections and Loans, Erin Gordon expertly handled all the logistics of moving this monumental work with Cayetana Castillo, Michael Hall, Ben Javellana, and Jessy Williams. Bob Ciesla in Facilities and Logistics; Lucio Ventura, Corey Burrage, and Joan Sullivan in Protection Services; and Peter Smiler in Visitor Services, along with their teams, were instrumental in presenting this work in our galleries.

Under the leadership of Francesca Casadio, the Conservation and Science team monitored the installation of this work in the museum, particularly Allison Langley, Elizabeth Wigfield, and Lisa Ackerman, along with their colleagues Isaac Facio, Kim Muir, and Julie Simek, as well as Joanna Shepard in London.

Richard J. Ferrer designed the exhibition, supervised by Samantha Grassi with Haiqa Nisar. In Experience Design, Gina Giambalvo, Logan Chappe, Kirill Mazor, and Alex Quintanilla produced the exhibition's digital content. Salvador Cruz, Erin Clark Fenton, and Kari McCluskey created the visual design and graphics.

In Interpretation, Ginia Shubik Sweeney ensured that the didactics were accessible as well as informative. Joe Iverson and Frances McMahon Ward created exciting public programs along with Katie Dyson and Jean Butler, assisted by Devin Davis, Rob Frye, Devonte Washington, Dan Wyche, and the team in Visitor Engagement, including Savanna Whelan and Leah Brecheisen. Sam Ramos and Nancy Chen creatively activated the galleries, while Jessica Alcazar, Emma Dreyfuss, Maura Flood, and Olivia Mendelson in the Ryan Learning Center mounted engaging programs for younger audiences.

Megan Michienzi, Lauren Schultz, Elizabeth Dudgeon, Nadine Schneller, Sadie Schwarm, and Salina Tsegai skillfully shared this artwork with the public. The Office of the President and Director, particularly Maureen Ryan, Claire Burdulis, and Kate Tierney Powell, was invaluably helpful. Jessica Applebee and Dawn Koster in Financial Planning and Analysis, Gaylene Burger in Accounting, and Troy Klyber in the Office of the General Counsel offered critical input. Anita Vigil guided this project for Philanthropy, while Stephanie Henderson, Caroline Avolio, Court Tan, and Zoe Berensztein created wonderful events.

Finally, *Raqib Shaw: Paradise Lost* would not have been possible without my steadfast colleagues in the Arts of Asia department, who stood behind this project from its inception. I am deeply thankful in particular to the Pritzker Chair of Arts of Asia, Curator of Chinese Art, and the Executive Director of Initiatives in Asia, Tao Wang, for his leadership and vision, and to Keely Morgan, who ably managed the many logistics. Miranda Ferries thoughtfully contributed at every stage. Matthew Alicea and Michael Solone expertly handled the installation, while Chi Nguyen and Randy Feeley offered behind-the-scenes administrative assistance.

I have been obsessed with Kashmir since I first visited the valley as a child with my mother. It is to the resilient people of this hauntingly beautiful place that I wish to dedicate this exhibition and publication, and to Raqib Shaw, for giving me the opportunity to revisit it. May it find the peace and tranquility that it richly deserves!

MADHUVANTI GHOSE
Alsdorf Associate Curator of Indian, Southeast Asian, and Himalayan Art
The Art Institute of Chicago

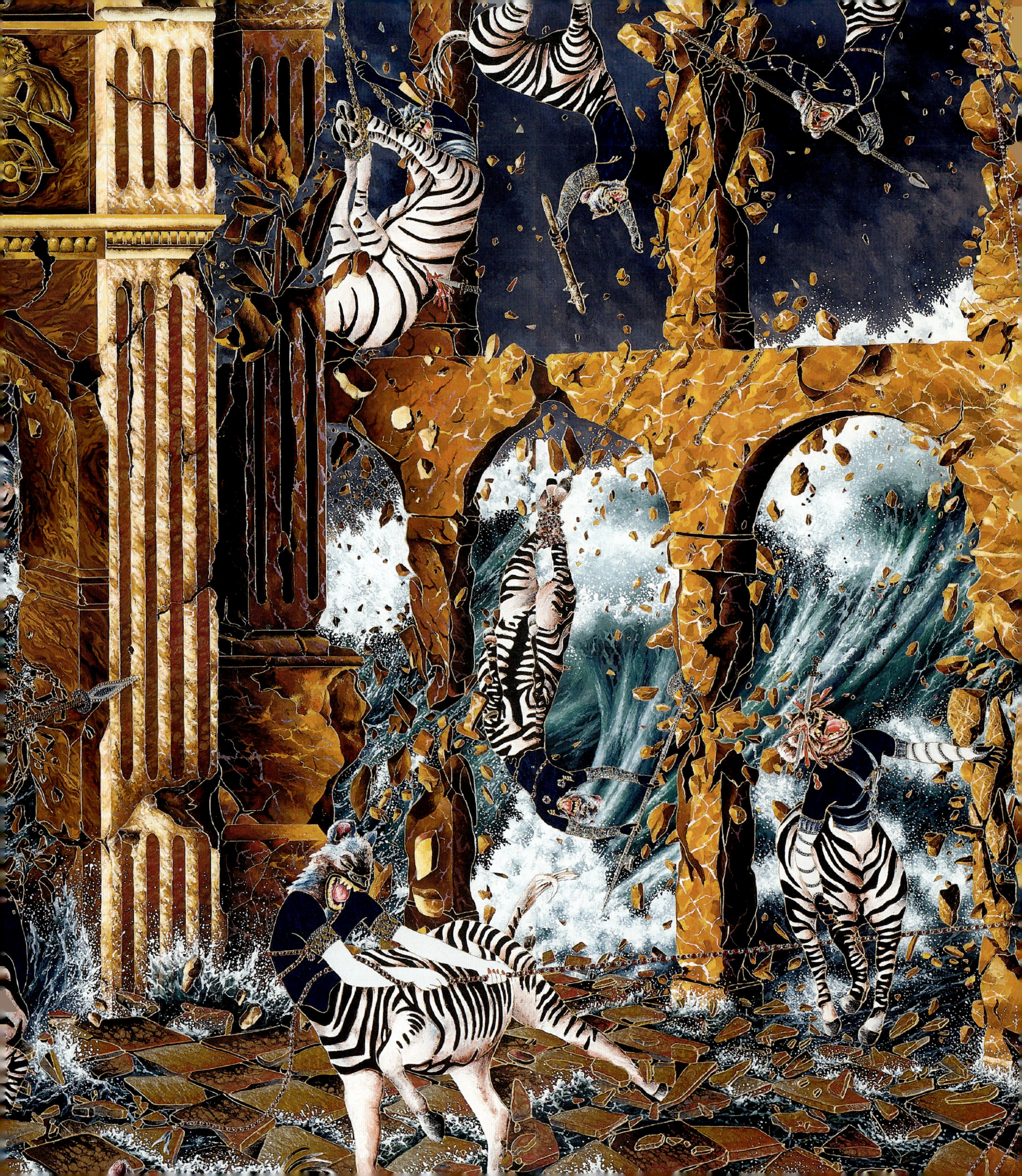

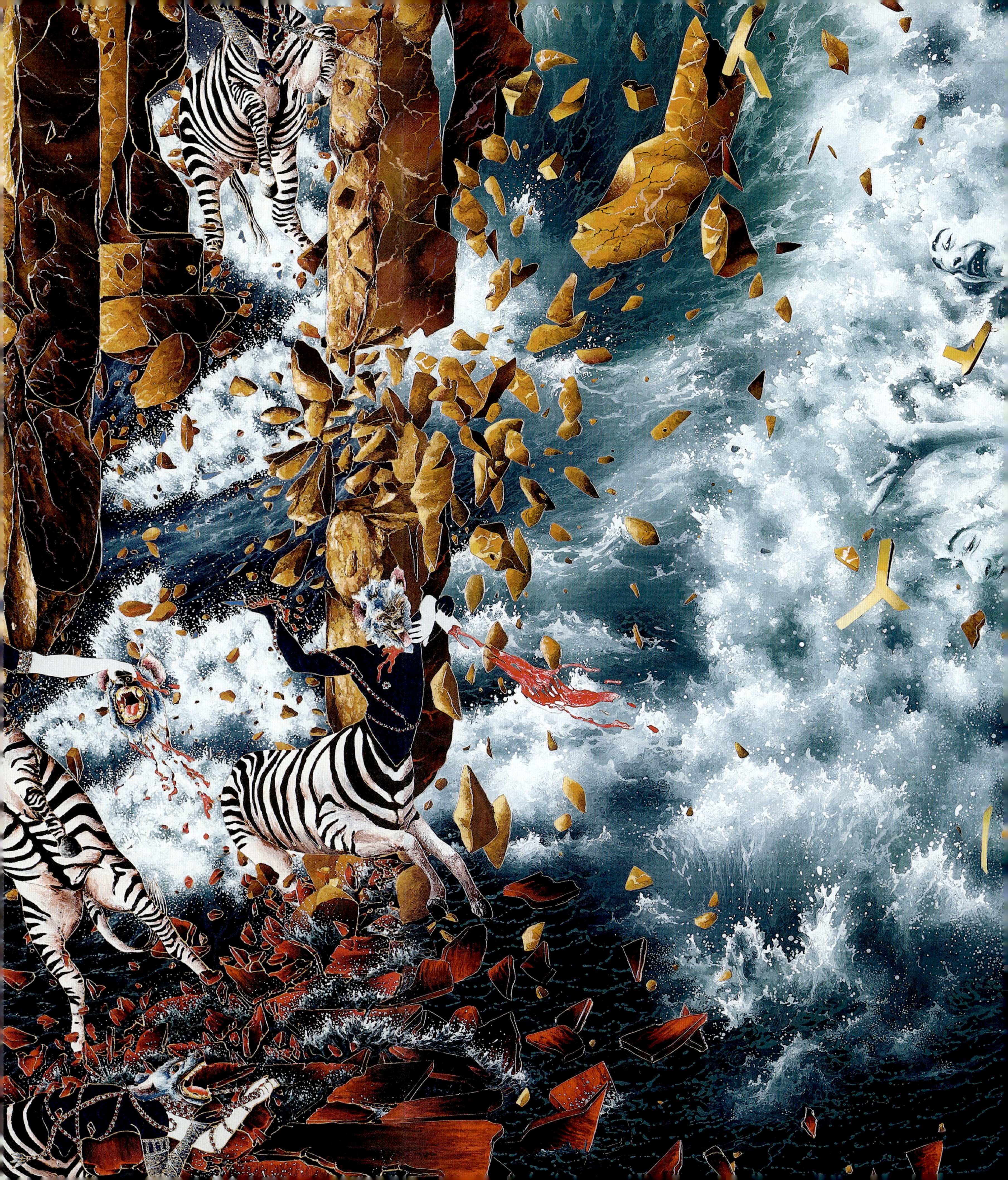

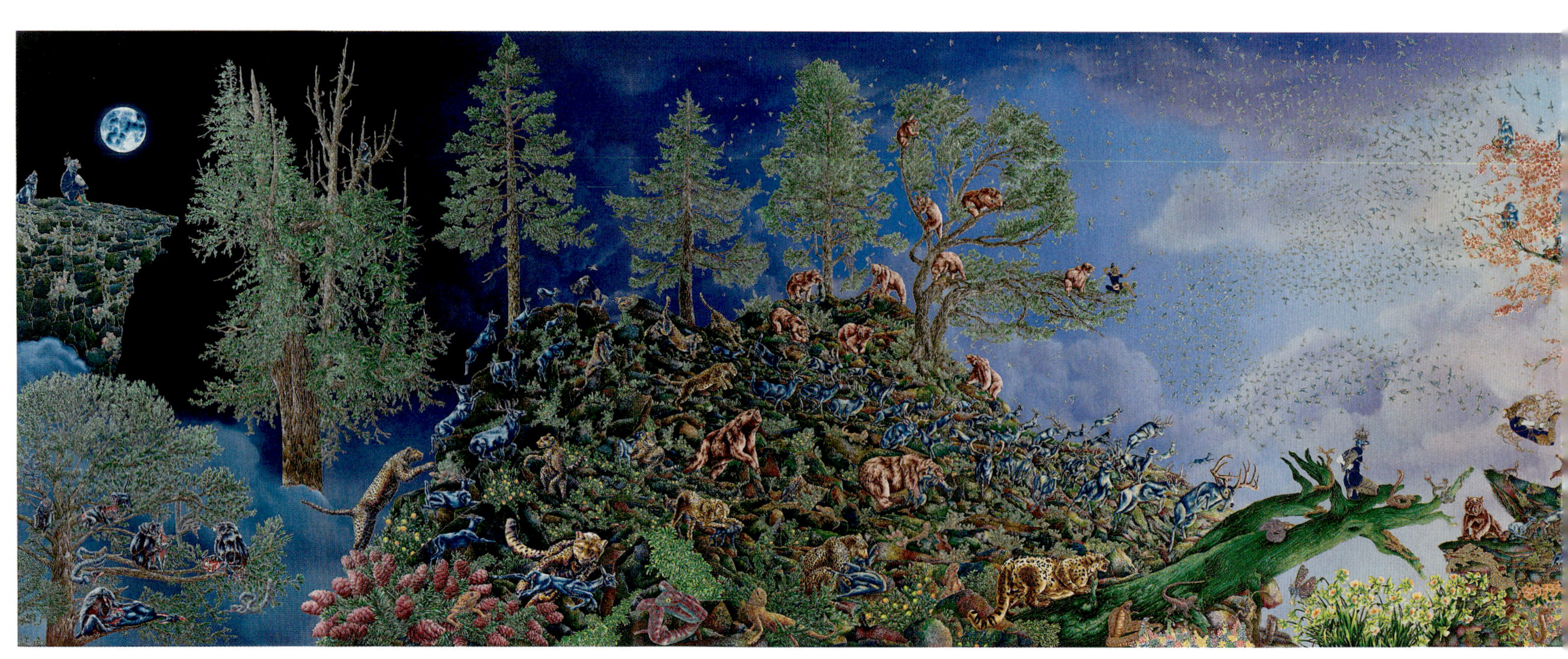

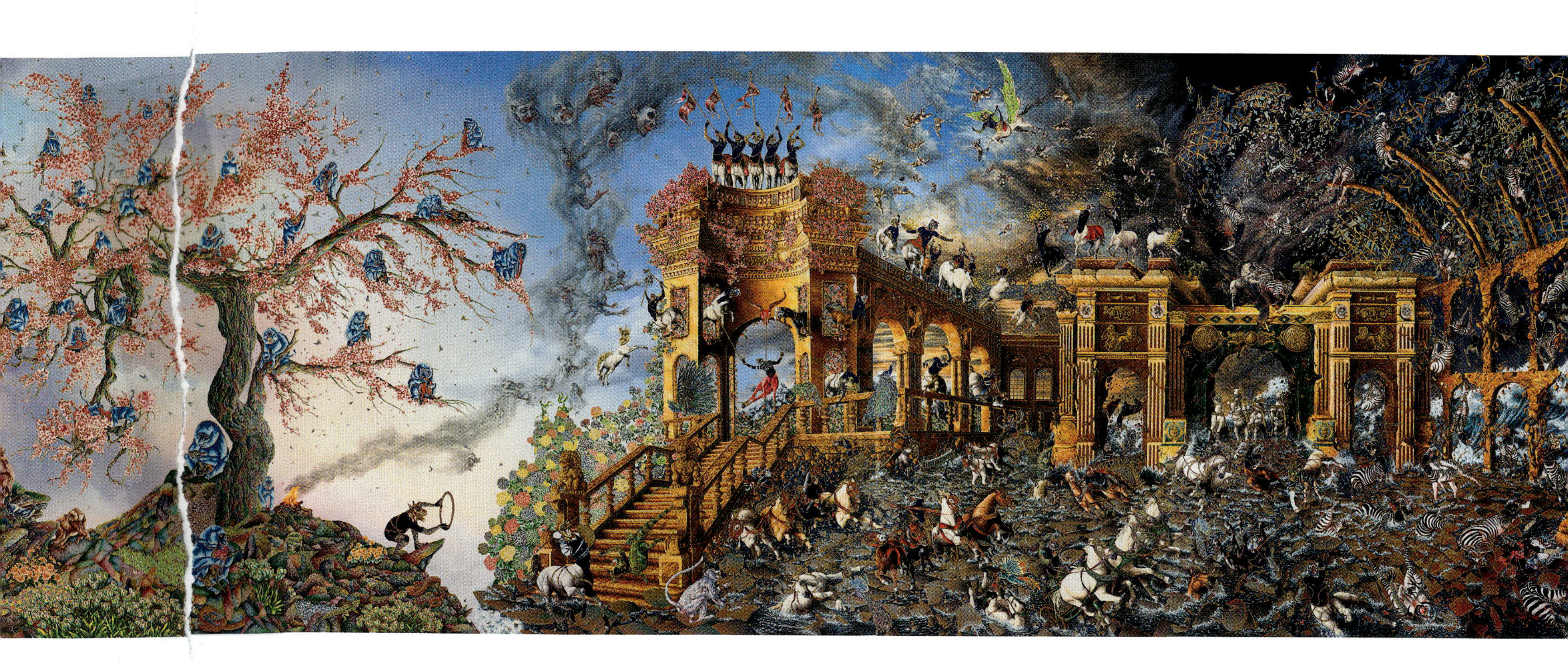

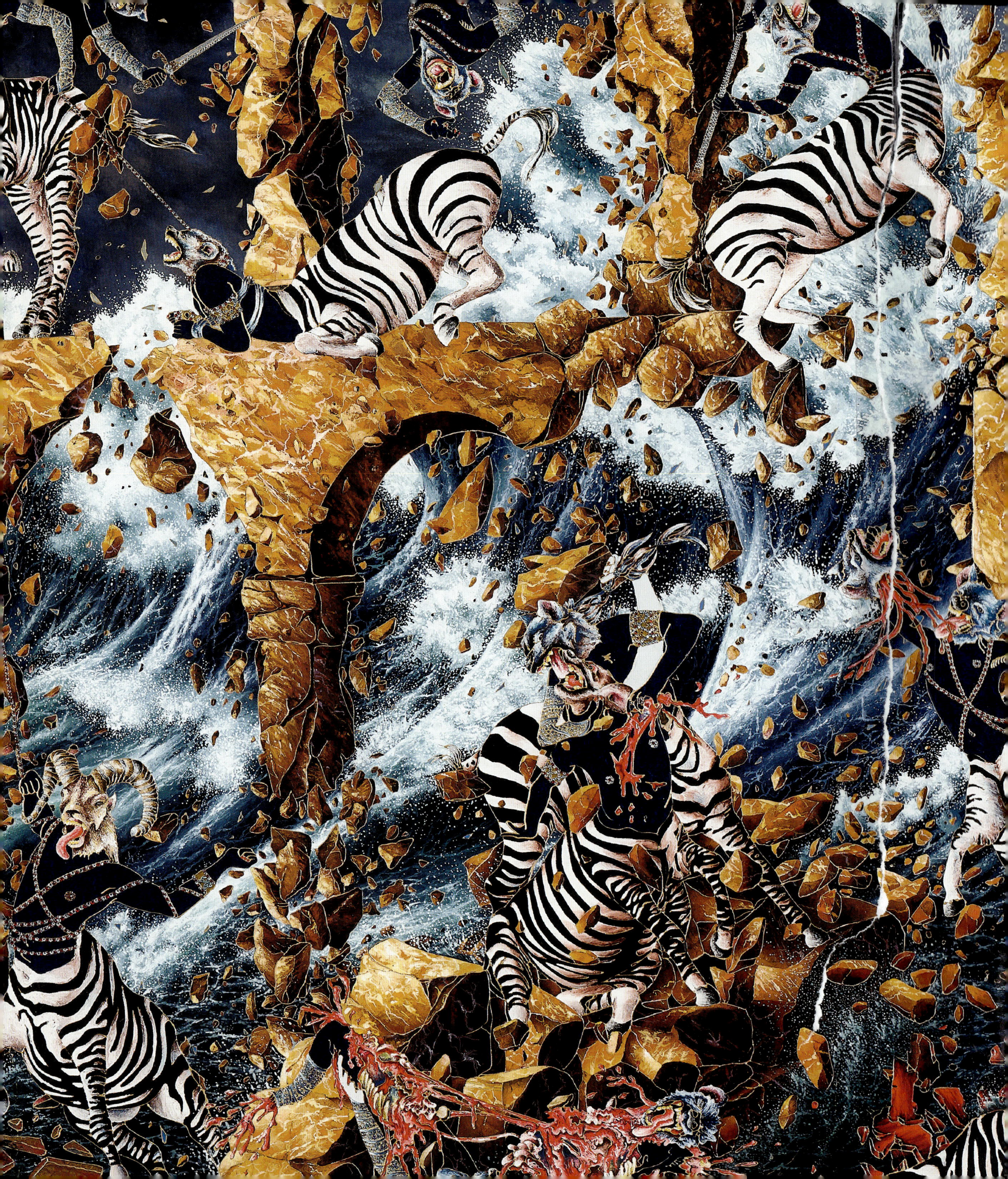

A Garden of Blissful Solitude
Painting, Reclusion, Paradise

David Lomas

You shall leave everything you love most dearly:
this is the arrow that the bow of exile shoots first.
—Dante, *Paradiso*, 17.55–57[1]

Reading from left to right, one does not advance very far into Raqib Shaw's multipanel painting *Paradise Lost* before coming upon the first inklings of discord. The first section alludes to the violence that has blighted his beloved homeland of Kashmir. A herd of deer scatter and flee in panic from marauding bears and leopards, while angry baboons tear apart bloodied carcasses and glare menacingly from overhead branches. A swarm of migratory swallows readying for departure gathers in the sky like a darkening storm cloud. A regal human-leopard hybrid perches on a rocky ledge and gazes across a chasm dividing two continents, one representing the past and the other an uncertain future. It is the artist in one of his varied avatars. Beneath his feet is a coiled serpent as he prepares to leave his once-Edenic homeland and embark on a one-way journey westward. A lived experience of migration, exile, and separation lies behind an epic narrative at the heart of which is the theme (or fantasy)—one that is achingly painful, but also generative—of a paradise lost.

Painting Pandemonium

The theme of paradise lost is most explicit in the second "chapter" of the painting, which comprises two subsections. In the first of these, a pitched battle ensues across a panorama like a cinema screen that engulfs the viewer. Shaw reinterpreted the classical subject of a battle between Lapiths and centaurs (fig. 1), symbolizing the combat between civilization and barbarity. Shaw's centaurs mostly have zebra stripes, and their upper bodies are animal-headed, compounding the creatures' animality and evincing a zeal for unnatural hybrids.[2] They brawl viciously among themselves. Amid the slaughter and mayhem, a row of bound zebrataurs dangle helplessly (fig. 2). Adding to the confusion, Roman chariots burst out of the picture, as if in a scene from *Ben-Hur*. The racing horses falter as the ground beneath them buckles and breaks up. All this frantic action occurs against an architectural backdrop of a grand staircase with a pair of Chinese guardian statues; in the center, a Piranesi-esque triumphal arch festooned with relief sculptures; and, to the right, the nave of a ruined Gothic cathedral. A mishmash of styles redolent of postmodernism, this structure is exploding and collapsing. A lattice glass ceiling shatters into a thousand shards as though the sky itself is falling.

Shaw has indicated that this section of the painting refers to the turbocharged London art world of the 1990s, a time of feverish speculation. Shaw was the golden boy gallerists were searching for: a newcomer whose edgy, exotic, and erotic painting was a welcome change from the thin gruel of abstract minimalism. *Garden of Earthly Delights III* (2003; private collection), from the series that propelled him to stardom, is a pleasure garden mirroring an art

1 Phidias (Greek, 500–430 BCE). Metope with Lapith and Centaur Fighting, c. 447–438 BCE. Marble; 122 × 132 cm (48 × 52 in.). British Museum, London.

2 Detail of *Paradise Lost* (see p. 49).

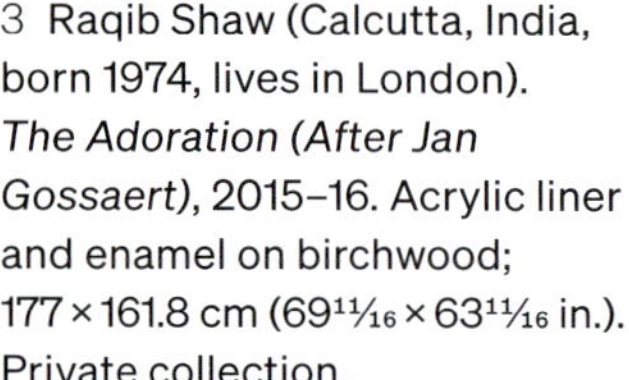

3 Raqib Shaw (Calcutta, India, born 1974, lives in London). *The Adoration (After Jan Gossaert)*, 2015–16. Acrylic liner and enamel on birchwood; 177 × 161.8 cm ($69\frac{11}{16} \times 63\frac{11}{16}$ in.). Private collection.

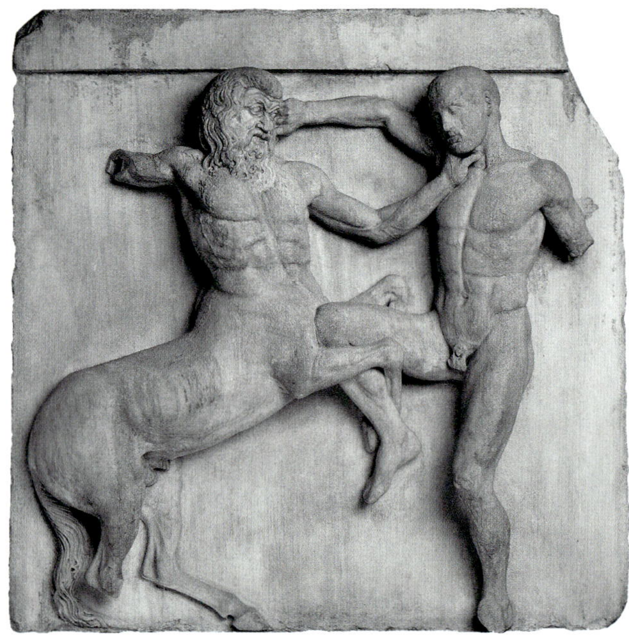

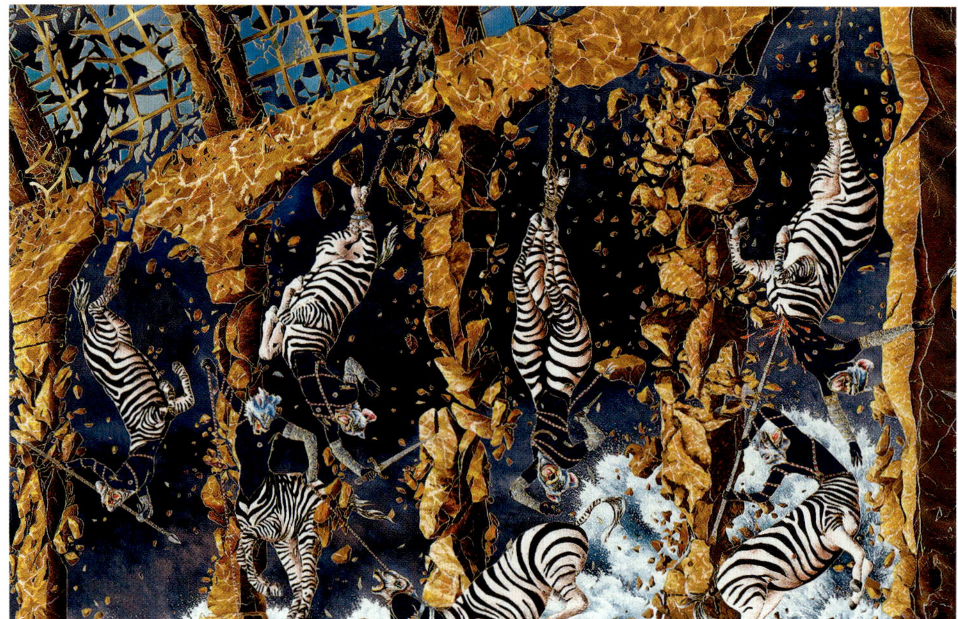

world drunk on hedonism. *Paradise Lost*, by contrast, is a hindsight view of that same world; a second take as Pandemonium, the capital of Hell in John Milton's *Paradise Lost*. With help from Satan's offsider, the demon Mammon, rebel angels constructed the city out of glittering gold.[3] *Pandemonium* well describes Shaw's dystopic vision of dog eating dog. Gold coins are showered like confetti, and the air is abuzz with brutish, ape-headed cupids signifying naked greed ("cupidity").[4] Looking beyond *Paradise Lost* to other works produced at the time, one discovers more evidence of a satirical take on the art world. In *The Adoration (After Jan Gossaert)* (fig. 3), the artist substituted himself for Mary, the mother of Jesus, and cradles his terrier, Mr C, on his lap. Dealers and collectors genuflecting to him are Magi but with the heads of jackals and hyenas.[5] Wringing his hands, Shaw proclaims: "*Vanitas vanitatum, omnia vanitas*" (vanity of vanities, all is vanity).

In *Paradise Lost*, the corrupted art world is about to be swept away by the force of a tsunami. The relevant passage in Milton's *Paradise Lost*, with its atmospheric evocation of the Biblical flood, looks ahead to a Roman aesthetic of sublime terror. Floating debris on a wild, foaming emerald sea is like the aftermath of a shipwreck. A Sotheby's sales catalogue, its cover adorned with one of Shaw's *Garden of Earthly Delights* paintings, floats near the bottom edge of the panel. The auction house on London's New Bond Street, one supposes, is one of those "Palaces / Where luxurie late reign'd" that now lies submerged on the ocean bed.[6]

Benjamin Britten's opera based upon *A Midsummer Night's Dream* inspired the pixies who aquaplane on the backs of regal swans before taking to the sky. Also mixed in are references to Ludwig II of Bavaria, the eccentric patron of Richard Wagner, whose sobriquet was the Swan King.[7] Shaw has claimed to channel the personality of Ludwig, with whom he has been obsessed for years.[8] Ludwig, who identified with Wagner's hero Lohengrin, had a rowboat with a gilt Eros mounted on the prow to

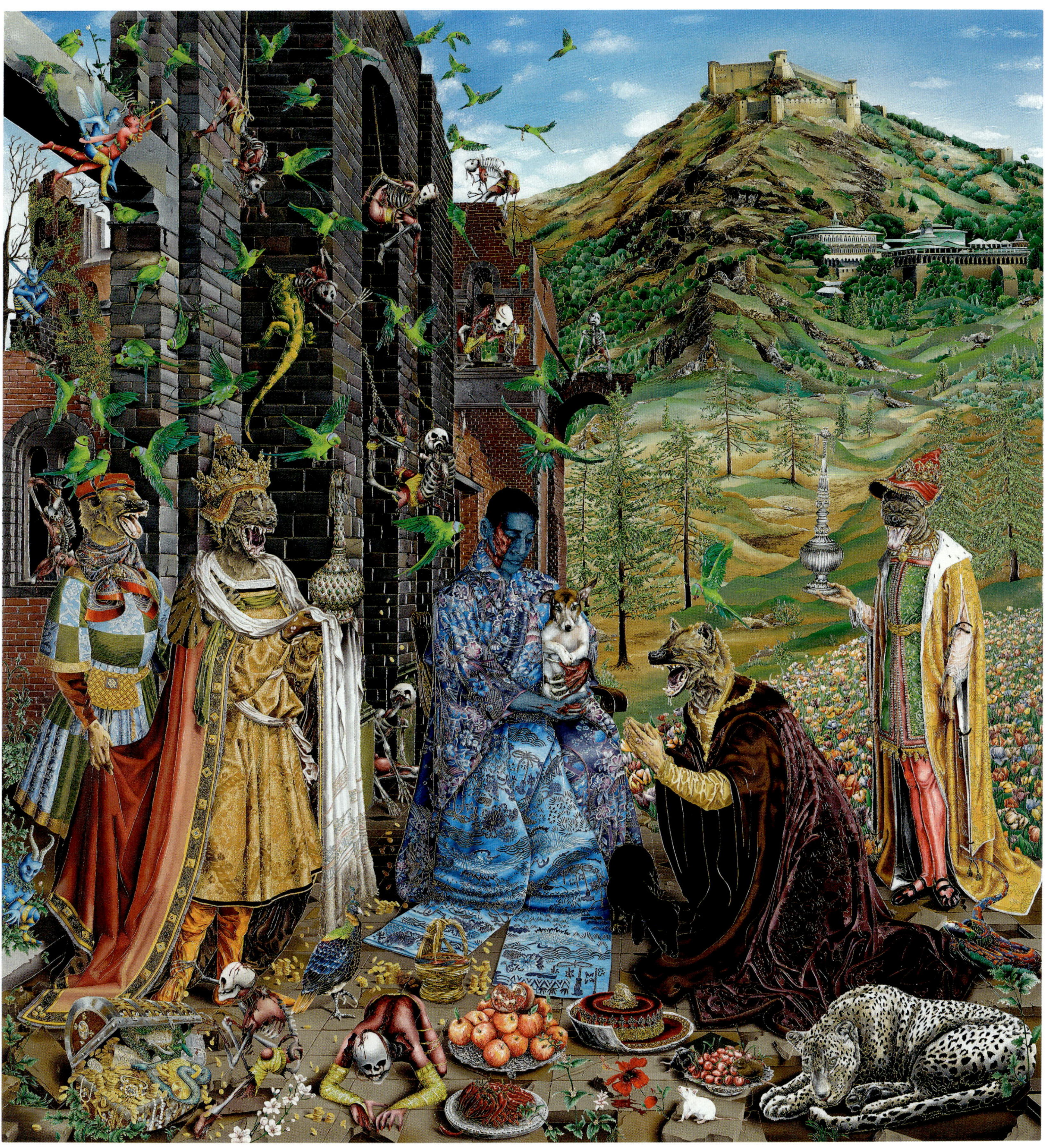

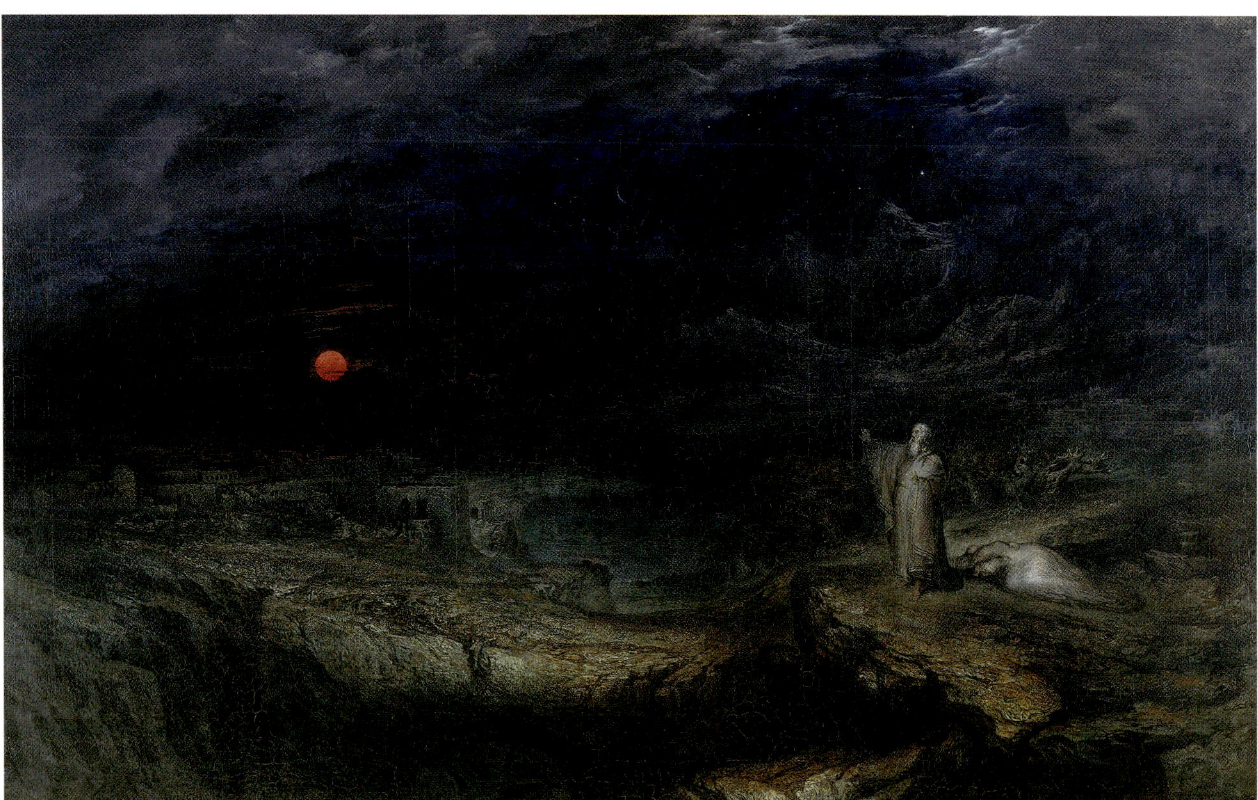

4 John Martin (British, 1789–1854). *The Last Man*, 1849. Oil on canvas; 137.8 × 214 cm (54¼ × 84¼ in.). Walker Art Gallery, Liverpool, UK.

convey him across a pond in an artificial grotto in the grounds of Linderhof Castle.[9] Its purpose here (see p. 52) may be, like Noah's ark, to ferry Shaw to safety. A copy of Pieter Brueghel's *Tower of Babel* (1563; Museum Boijmans Van Beuningen, Rotterdam, Netherlands) looms unexpectedly in the background of this section (see p. 51). Perhaps it refers to the postmodern art world that greeted the newly graduated artist, a confusing Babel of artistic languages in which one could either sink or learn to swim.

The Last Man

During the first voyage of Sinbad the Sailor, one of the tales in *The Thousand and One Nights*, Sinbad is the only survivor of a shipwreck. Perched atop a barrel with his legs dangling in the water, he is borne by driving winds and waves through night and all the next day before making landfall on an uncharted island.[10] We spot Shaw, like Sinbad, stretched out prostrate on a rocky ledge, a centaur behind him gesturing defiantly at the apocalypse he has luckily escaped (see pp. 52–53). Shaw, barely alive on a foreign shore, represents the nadir of the painter's own spiritual journey.

John Martin's *The Last Man* (fig. 4), a picture of likely interest to Shaw, reverses the biblical topos of Adam in paradise as the first man. It is a baleful image of a bearded patriarch on a bare rocky outcrop, his raised arm reaching out toward a dying, entropic sun, with the naked corpses of a woman and child at his feet.[11] Martin was frowned upon as a purveyor of potboilers in the apocalyptic genre, but his work has seen a dramatic turnaround in critical fortunes owing to its resonances with our own end-times. His brooding, velvety black mezzotint prints of *Paradise Lost* are among the best-known illustrations of Milton's poem. Martin also created a standalone painting, *Pandemonium* (1841; Musée du Louvre, Paris), in which a river of lava flows past a building based on plans for the new Houses of Parliament in Westminster. Martin was inclined to view London as a modern Pandemonium, albeit for other reasons than Shaw.[12]

A solitary figure contemplating the immensity of nature is a stock motif in Romanticism, exemplified by Caspar David Friedrich's iconic painting of a

5 Caspar David Friedrich (German, 1774–1840). *Forest Interior by Moonlight*, 1823–30. Oil on canvas; 70.5 × 49 cm (27½ × 19¼ in.). Alte Nationalgalerie, Berlin.

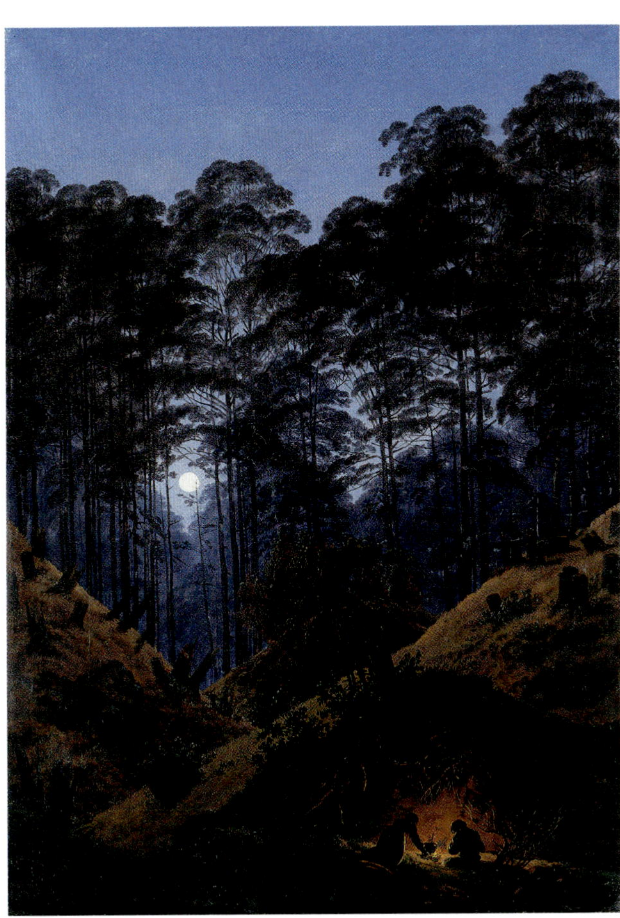

wanderer high in the mountains gazing across a sea of cloud.[13] Loneliness is exalted, especially as it fosters a sense of communion with nature. The notion of *Einfühlung*—literally a "feeling into" nature, coined within the field of aesthetics by Robert Vischer, and subsequently translated into English as "empathy"—expresses a pantheistic oneness with nature that is repeatedly invoked by Shaw and is the crux of his concept of paradise. In Friedrich's *Forest Interior by Moonlight* (fig. 5), the glow of a centrally placed full moon filters through a flat screen of conifer trees in a lonely alpine landscape. At the front of the picture, composed of interlocking triangular wedges of earth denuded of trees by the winds, two travelers have lit a fire and taken refuge in a cave-like overhang left by an uprooted tree. While moonlit landscapes were popular in seventeenth-century Dutch painting, Friedrich made the moon the subject, an object of rapt contemplation by lonely figures within the painting.[14] A fervent disciple of Romanticism, Shaw extols solitariness, likening it to

> melancholic music, songs of sorrow, all that is tinged with sadness brought about by fleeting yet heart-stopping beauty, be it the last moments of an expiring sunset or the gust of wind that steals the last cherry blossom away, robbing the tree of its youth. Or that last glance knowing that you will not see [again] the vision of what was once the most loved.[15]

Proceeding onward, we next encounter Shaw as a hermit cloaked in a Kashmiri shawl. He shelters in a hut in the middle of a forest clearing, alone apart from wild goats and leopards (see p. 53).[16] The rudimentary stone and thatch dwelling is of a type used by nomadic herders, the Gujjars and Bakarwals, who graze their animals high in the Himalayan mountains in the summer, descending to lower terrain in the winter.[17] This vignette harkens back to Shaw's appearance in the first panel, before leaving Kashmir, squatting on haunches in a forest staring transfixed at a full moon with only a wolf for a companion.

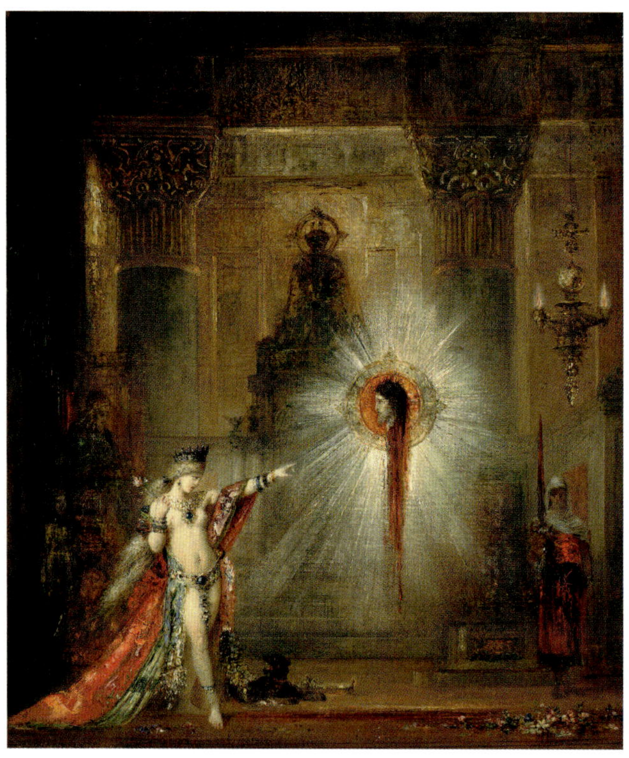

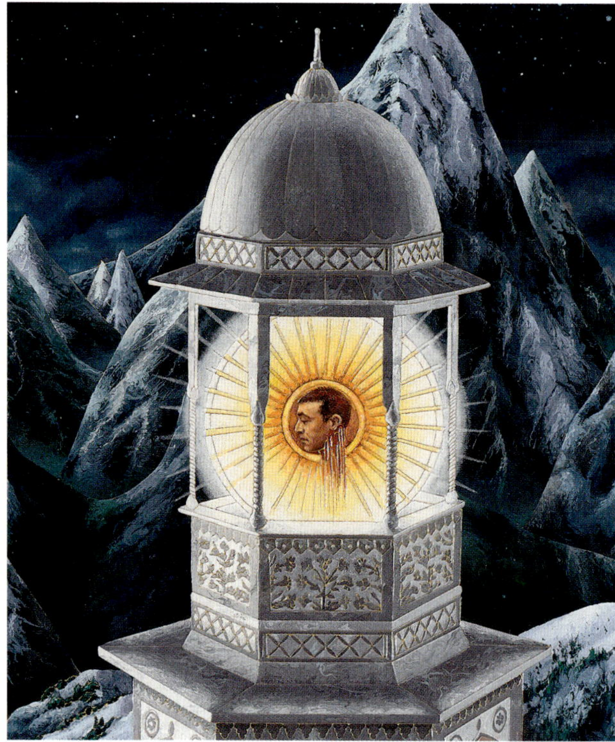

6 Gustave Moreau (French, 1826–1898). *The Apparition*, c. 1876–77. Oil on canvas; 55.9 × 46.7 cm (22 × 18⅜ in.). Harvard Art Museums/ Fogg Museum, Bequest of Grenville L. Winthrop, 1943.268.

7 Detail of *Paradise Lost* (see p. 52).

On Reclusion

When I quizzed Shaw about reclusion, which had struck me as a pervasive impulse while surveying his recent work, it prompted an impassioned outpouring from him. "My whole existence," he wrote, "is embalmed in the resin of reclusion, caused by the phenomenon of reclusion. In the midst of a hundred people, this affliction of reclusion intensifies. Only bees, birds, flowers, and nature bring some respite to this—seemingly superficial, conceptually empty—condition that easily fills up the soul leaving absolutely no room for anything else but allows only tools of its own worship to heighten its presence, to bring focus to its mighty monotheistic majority."[18] Reclusion was embraced by late nineteenth-century Symbolist artists and writers whom Shaw regards as existential soulmates. Jean Des Esseintes, the dandyish hero of Joris-Karl Huysmans's cult novel *À Rebours* (*Against Nature*), epitomizes the type. Repelled by the materialism of bourgeois modernity, Des Esseintes decamps from Paris to the suburbs where he finds consolation in monastic seclusion. Huysmans devotes a lengthy ekphrasis to Gustave Moreau's *Apparition* (fig. 6), a prized possession adorning Des Esseintes's apartment.[19] It is one of Moreau's many variant compositions of the beheading of Saint John the Baptist. Salome, bedecked with jewelry, struts regally before the lascivious Herod. She holds aloft a lotus flower, a symbol of purity, as the head of John, dripping blood, materializes before her. Purloined by Shaw, it reappears in a tower that rears up out of the sea like a lighthouse in the central section of *Paradise Lost*, his own profile pointedly substituted for that of the sacrificial saint (fig. 7).

With pictures titled *The Perseverant Prophet*, *The Mystic Soothsayer*, *The Estranged Foreigner*, *The Erudite Hermit*, *The Penitent Sage*, and *The Mourning Mendicant*, Shaw testifies to his impulse toward hermit-like reclusion and the solace afforded by solitude.[20] Common to these works is an ambiguous interplay between vision and reality. Whole cityscapes erupt from the floor or hover mysteriously in the sky. It certainly looks as though Shaw has been studying René Magritte. He conjured with interior and exterior space, replacing an entire wall or floor with a touristic vista of Venice or a Kashmiri forest; what appears to be a wall mirror does not reflect but gives onto another landscape. The web of citation and cross-reference is extremely dense. Within these

8 Odilon Redon (French, 1840–1916). *Buddha*, 1904. Distemper on canvas; 159.8 × 121.1 cm (63 × 47¾ in.). Van Gogh Museum, Amsterdam.

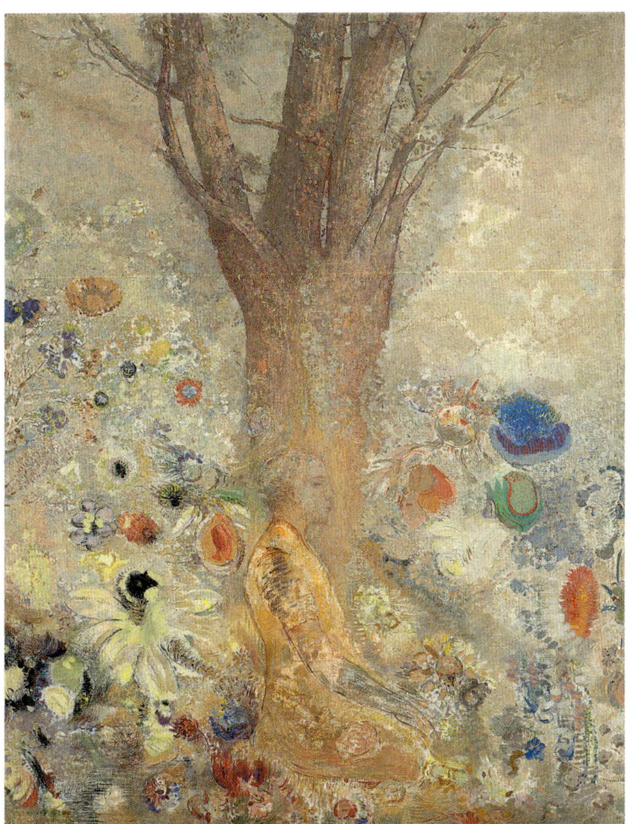

parallel universes of uncertain reality, the artist himself is liable to appear more than once, frequently viewed from behind in a manner that overtly recalls the soulful monk or solitary wanderer of a Friedrich landscape. The figure of the artist is the only unifying element in these pictures, tethering us to reality where little solid ground exists. Such considerations deserve to be borne in mind when looking at *Paradise Lost*, where a similar ontological uncertainty pertains to the subject of paradise itself: Is it dream or reality?

Late nineteenth-century artists and writers reacted to the rampant materialism of their era by adopting aspects of Eastern spirituality. Severing worldly attachments is seen as a prerequisite to the attainment of enlightenment. Buddha, at the crucial turning point in his journey, dismounts from his horse, bids farewell to his footman, and exchanges his fine garments for the plain robes of a mendicant monk. Odilon Redon depicted Buddha in profile meditating beneath a tree whose trunk merges with his body, surrounded by flowers (fig. 8).[21] The Bodhi tree is a sacred fig (*Ficus religiosa*) beneath which Buddha sat when he attained enlightenment. Shaw emulated this archetypal motif in a realistic self-portrait marooned on a tiny island at the midpoint of *Paradise Lost* (see p. 51). Wrapped in a Kashmiri shawl and seated at the base of a cherry tree, he exudes the equanimity of a sage or prophet. Seen in dialogue with this portrait, the seas raging all about him correspond on a cosmic scale to the purgation that he privately undergoes at this midway point of his pilgrimage.

Themes of reclusion are prevalent in Chinese art at certain historical periods, notably when China came under Mongol rule. Rather than serve in the new regime, officials might choose reclusion and devote themselves to painting, calligraphy, and poetry.[22] One consequence is that goodbyes and embarkation on a journey have a salience in Chinese art and poetry that they do not possess in the West. Amid a welter of other cultural references, we should not overlook an influence of Chinese painting: Shaw calls forth a formal kinship with Chinese scroll painting in the horizontal format of *Paradise Lost*.[23]

A Cult of Art

Renunciation goes hand in hand with reclusion. Penitence through privation or the infliction of physical pain is depicted in the paintings of Christian saints. Saint Jerome strikes his chest with a rock in imitation of Christ's suffering (*imitatio Christi*) while contemplating the Crucifixion. Saint Sebastian, with whom Shaw also has said he identifies, luxuriates in the exquisite pain of his martyrdom in a painting (c. 1623) by Gerrit van Honthorst in London's National Gallery. Freud recognized something similar in states of mourning and melancholia where the superego remorselessly punishes the ego, or self. The culmination of Shaw's self-abnegation is a self-portrait titled *The Final Submission in Fire on Ice* (fig. 9). It is like the record of a performance, depicting the artist somber and downcast, consigning to flames his precious embroidered shawl, a keepsake and material token of home and his Kashmiri identity. Mourning seeks ultimately to detach the subject from a loved but now lost object. A pronounced mournfulness suffuses an entire body of predominantly wintry scenes, notably Shaw's variations on Lucas Cranach's *Melancholy* (1532; Statens Museum for Kunst, Copenhagen, Denmark). Shaw stages quite literally a "death of the author" in *Last Rites of the Artist's Ego at Shankaracharya Temple (After Ludovico Mazzolino)* (2015–16; private collection), a Poe-like representation of himself mobbed by black ravens as he reads the last rites to a body double laid out in an open coffin. The setting is an isolated temple in Srinagar in the depths of winter.

Saint Jerome is venerated for translating the Bible into Latin, a labor of love that became his life's work. *The Golden Legend*, a medieval sourcebook, records that Jerome returned to Bethlehem after four years in the desert: "And there he assembled many disciples unto him for to labor there in his holy purpose, and abode there in the translation of holy Scripture fifty-five years and six months, and remained a pure virgin unto the end of his life."[24] When Shaw takes the place of Saint Jerome, as he does repeatedly, whether it is in the studio or penitent in the wilderness, he decouples the subject from its religious meaning. Art, not religion, is the ideal to which he is dedicated. Shaw has represented himself at a desk like Jerome; instead of Jerome's tame lion, his attribute is a Himalayan snow leopard. One imagines him poring over the art history books piled at his feet and communing with the European artists he admires: Bosch, Brueghel, Cranach, Van Eyck, Piranesi, and Tintoretto. He reads Giorgio Vasari's *Lives of the Artists* with the fervor of a monk studying the lives of saints. In one of his versions of this subject, the setting is his studio in south London; in another he is transported as if on a magic carpet back to his idealized homeland in the Himalayas. Like Jerome or Saint Anthony, Shaw's self-portrait is tempted by lubricious visions but remains steadfast and commendably unmoved. Shaw incorporated an engraving by Martin Schongauer of Saint Anthony in midair assailed by fantastical hybrid demons into the *Winter* panel of his *Four Seasons* (2018–19; private collection), with the artist usurping the place of the bearded saint.[25]

Shaw's work resurrects a cult of art and beauty last associated with the English Pre-Raphaelites and their successors in the Aesthetic movement. His studio, formerly a sausage factory, is akin to a monastery where everyone is wholly dedicated to the religion of art. Witnessing the hushed concentration, my

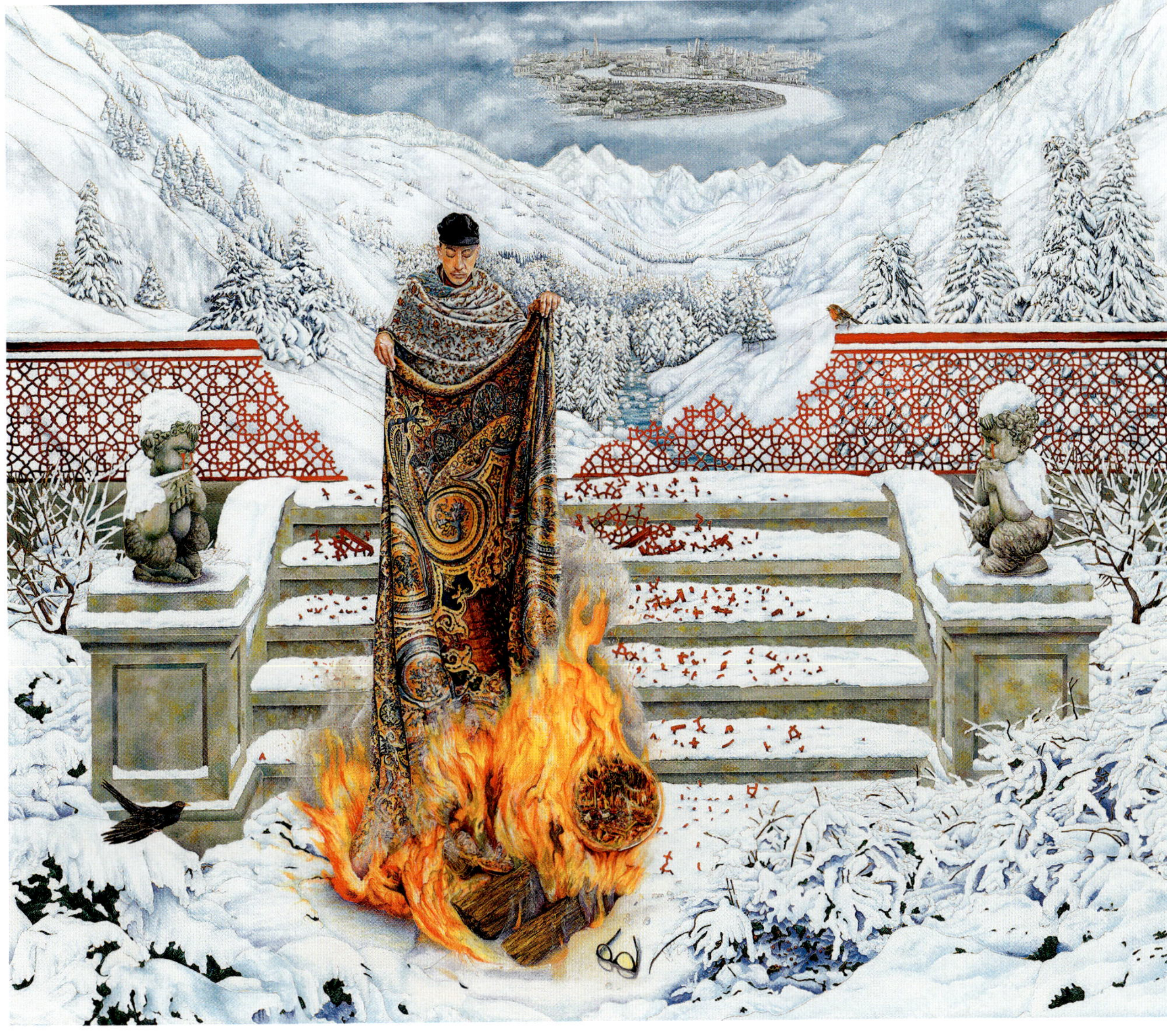

9 Raqib Shaw. *The Final Submission in Fire on Ice*, 2021–22. Acrylic liner and enamel on aluminum; 97.4 × 110 cm (38⅜ × 43¼ in.). National Portrait Gallery, London.

thoughts turn to the eleventh-century workshop in Canterbury where the *Bayeux Tapestry* (Bayeux Tapestry Museum, France)—at two hundred feet in length, a supreme example of narrative art—was embroidered.[26] In a number of pictures, a colonnaded wall interposes a barrier between the outside world and a cloistered, quasi-sacred space of artistic creation. The *Madonna of Chancellor Rolin* (1400–50; Musée du Louvre, Paris) by Jan van Eyck, revered as the inventor of oil painting, may have inspired this compositional device. The studio, thus segregated from the profane world, is an ideal milieu for artistically recreating paradise.

What should one make of Icarus at the right edge of *Paradise Lost* (who also appears in *From Narcissus to Icarus . . . A Summer Odyssey*; fig. 12) plunging from the sky to a certain death? In mythology, Icarus flew up to the heavens on wings made by his father, the carpenter Daedalus, but the heat of the sun melted the wax attaching feathers to his arms. Icarus is punished for hubris in daring to encroach upon the heavenly realm that is the abode of the gods. In Milton's *Paradise Lost*, the fall of the rebel angels cast out of heaven is a moment of drama and pathos: "Hurld headlong flaming from th' Ethereal Skie / With hideous ruine and combustion down / To bottomless perdition."[27] The Islamic culture in which Shaw was raised was rich in decorative arts, but there were very few paintings. It wasn't until he went to Britain and visited the National Gallery that he saw European

10 Lucas Cranach the Elder (German, 1472–1553). *The Garden of Eden*, 1530. Oil on limewood; 118 × 80 cm (46½ × 31½ in.). Gemäldegalerie Alte Meister, Dresden.

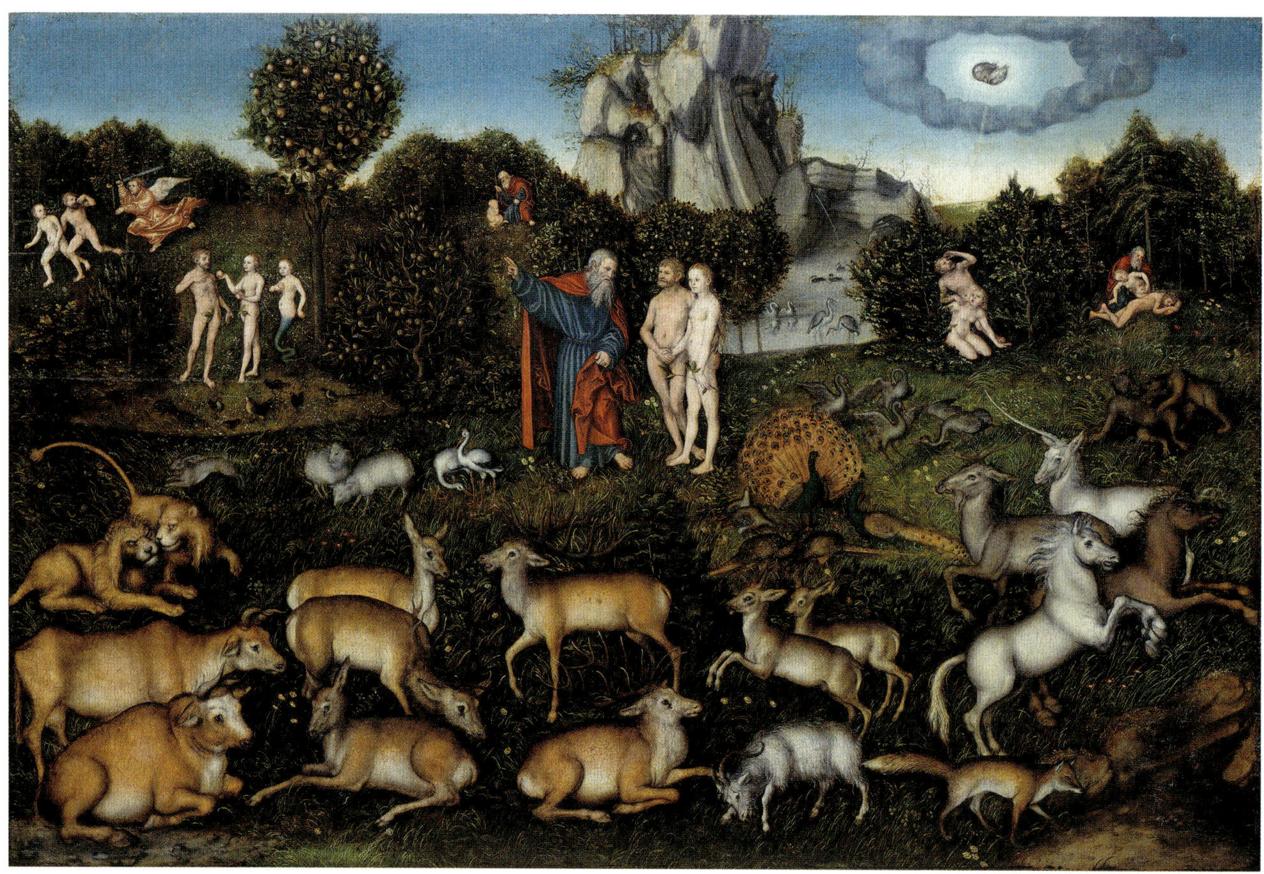

paintings for the first time and resolved to become an artist. He has described Hans Holbein the Younger's *Ambassadors* (1533) as a revelation.[28] As an avatar of the artist, Icarus expresses the ambition to be the equal of those immortals, to create something of enduring beauty, but it also contains perhaps a residue of an ancient prohibition against images and of the punishment for transgression.[29]

Landscape and Place

Etymologically, the word *paradise* migrated from East to West. Its original meaning, "enclosed garden," referred to walled parks where royal hunts took place. Xenophon of Athens adopted the Old Iranian *paridaiza* into Greek as *paradeisos*, the word employed for the Garden of Eden in Greek editions of the Old Testament. From his first major series, *Garden of Earthly Delights*, paradise has been a leitmotif of Shaw's work, invariably connected with the Kashmir homeland he left behind.

The most Edenic of Shaw's paintings, *The Dream* (2018–22; private collection), is a hallucinatory flashback to a fondly remembered Kashmir conjured in an illusionistic technique that makes the nostalgic fantasy almost real. It has numerous correspondences with the *Garden of Eden* by Lucas Cranach (fig. 10). A herd of deer graze on the edges of a stream under moonlight, in the midst of which we encounter the artist writing poetry beneath a cherry tree, an image that is reprised in the deluge panel of *Paradise Lost*. The deer are untroubled by the ferocious predators that cause them to scatter in the first chapter of Shaw's *Paradise Lost*. In a departure from the conventional imagery of Adam and Eve in the Garden of Eden, Shaw in his paintings is nearly always alone apart from the animals that keep him company. A pair of partridges, adapted from Vincenzo Catena's *Saint Jerome in His Study* (c. 1475; National Gallery, London), and a nonchalant hare nestle close by the artist. The only thing to disturb this idyll is a coiled serpent in the right foreground.

Landscape is first and foremost a representation of place. The experience of exile is registered in landscape as a discordant sense of physical and psychological displacement and dislocation. In his seminal essay "Reflections on Exile," Edward Said adopted a musical term, *contrapuntal*, referring to the intertwining of two or more melodies, to describe the bifurcated reality of the exile.[30] We recognize this duality in Shaw's landscape imagery as the simultaneous copresence of a here and an elsewhere. Perception and memory mingle in a sort of double vision. Shaw has borrowed from the Northern European tradition of the world landscape, a genre pioneered by Joachim Patinir, reflecting knowledge of a world that had grown exponentially in extent due to travel and exploration.[31] Deep recession and a high horizon line are typical features of this tradition as are dramatic rock formations arising from the ocean like wondrous new continents. Themes of journeying and exile are readily associated with the world landscape, as seen in Pieter Brueghel the Elder's *Landscape with the Flight into Egypt* (1563; Courtauld Gallery, London).

Shaw's *From Amarnath to Alderbrook* (2016–17; Usha Mittal Collection) displays the contrapuntal rhythm that Said associated with the experience of exile. Amarnath is an important Hindu pilgrimage site dedicated to Shiva in Kashmir; Alderbrook is the country estate in Surrey where Shaw planned a fantastical garden. The panoramic vista across a broad valley to mountains beyond recapitulates Shaw's personal journey from one to the other. The elevated vantage point in this picture, typical of the world landscape, produces a sense of detachment from the earth, and from a grounded place within it. The work of the work, so to speak, is not just to bridge two geographically separated places. Subjectively, and more importantly, it is to reconnect Shaw's past with his present. A Himalayan range similar to that in the distance of *From Amarnath to Alderbrook* stretches across the deluge scene of *Paradise Lost*. Towering above the roiling sea, it is a reassuringly fixed compass point indelibly etched upon Shaw's psyche.

For the exiled, memories of the past intrude with a force that hollows out the present. Shaw has conveyed the omnipresence of memory in a direct and efficacious manner by means of thought bubbles, such as one sees to the right of the artist marooned on a tiny island in the deluge scene. A scene referencing *From Amarnath to Alderbrook* appears as a large floating bubble at this pivotal juncture (fig. 11). Thought bubbles convey with the immediacy of a comic book what is going on in the artist's head, often a sense of melancholy or loss. Formally, they are a picture-within-a-picture, and most of them are excerpts—in quotation marks, as it were—from other of his artworks, reinforcing the threads of connection between them.

Dancing with Daffodils

The English Romantic poetry that Shaw has read avidly since his schooldays has nurtured a reverence

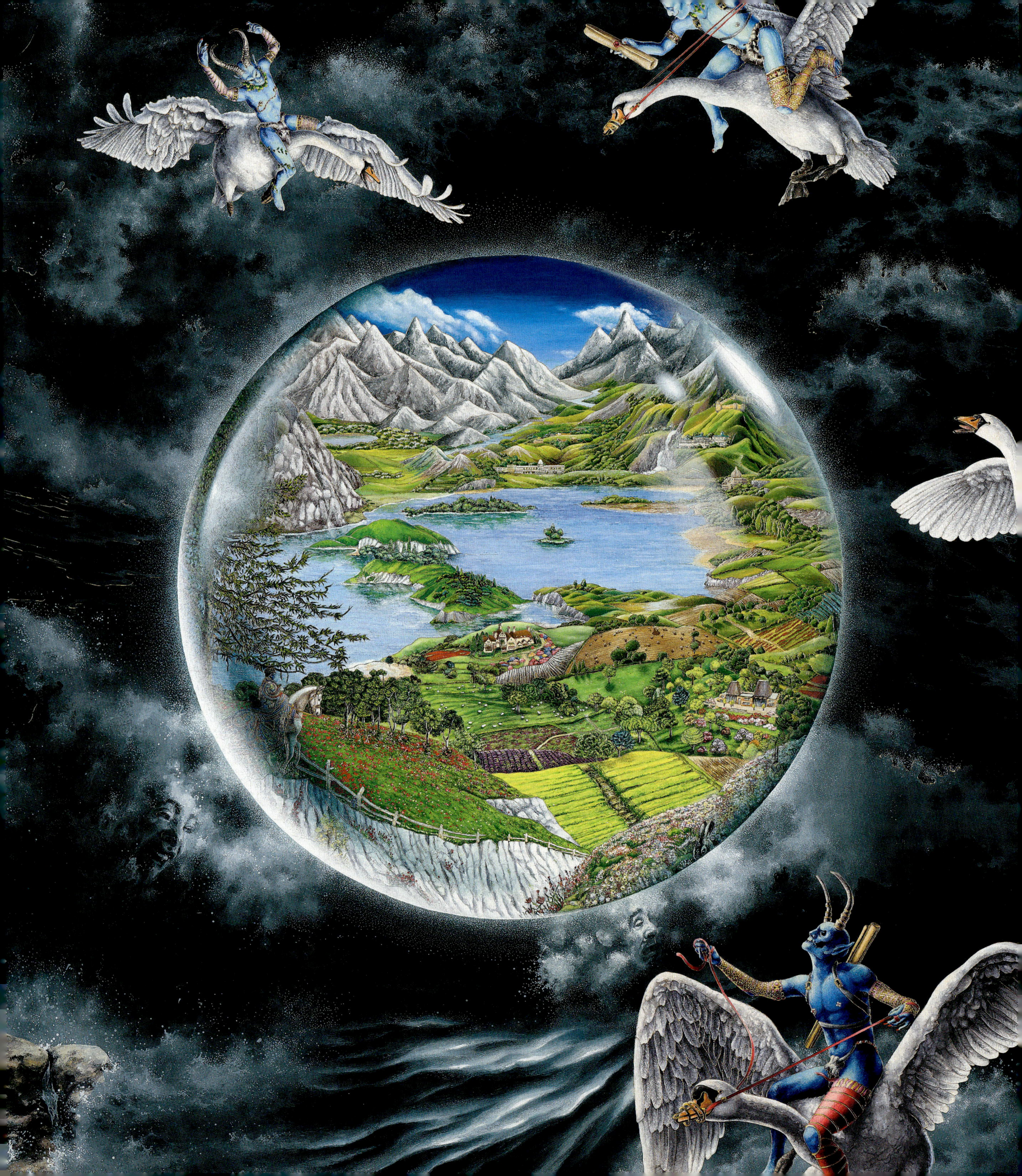

11 Detail of *Paradise Lost* (see p. 51).

12 Raqib Shaw. *From Narcissus to Icarus . . . A Summer Odyssey*, 2016–18. Acrylic liner and enamel on aluminum; 247.1 × 330 cm (97¼ × 129¹⁵⁄₁₆ in.). Usha Mittal Collection.

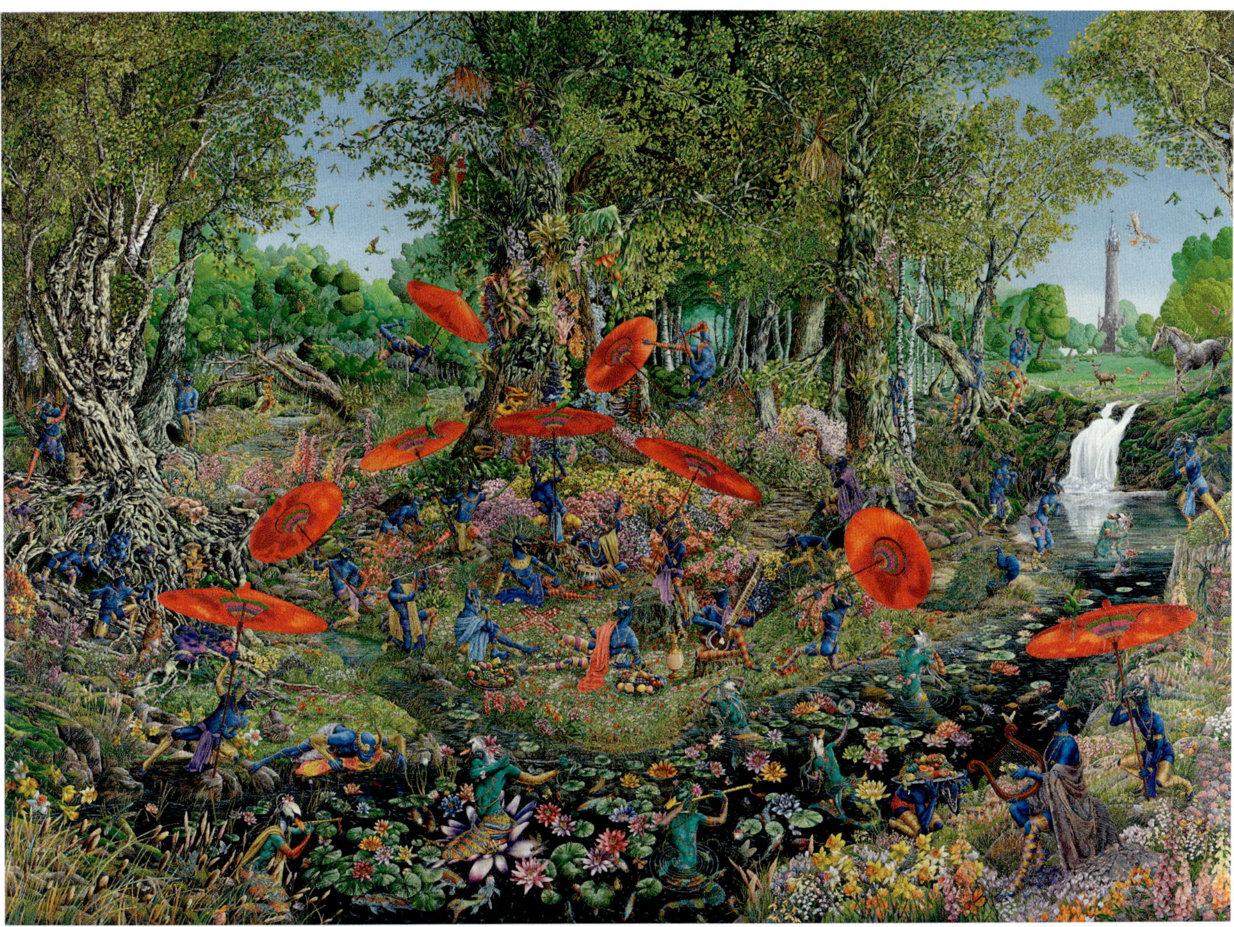

for nature. William Wordsworth's ever-popular verse, "I Wandered Lonely as a Cloud," describes the poet as he is strolling beside Ullswater in the Lake District and catches sight of daffodils at the water's edge, "fluttering and dancing in the breeze." Recalled later in "the bliss of solitude," this image still retains its power to uplift the poet:

> For oft, when on my couch I lie
> In vacant or in pensive mood,
> They flash upon that inward eye
> Which is the bliss of solitude;
> And then my heart with pleasure fills,
> And dances with the daffodils.[32]

From Narcissus to Icarus . . . A Summer Odyssey (fig. 12), Shaw's riff on Édouard Manet's *Dejeuner sur l'herbe* (1863; Musée d'Orsay, Paris), radiates a joyous, pantheistic spirit. The central figure group, emulating Manet's composition, relax in the sunshine and are entertained by a troupe of dancers and musicians. In a move that effects a radical *dépaysement* of the source image, wrenching it from its place in histories of European art, Shaw populated his version with peacock-headed figures in cobalt-blue tights sumptuously bedecked with jewelry. The lithe athleticism of these characters, recalling Moreau's Salome, is unmistakably Indian in inspiration.

Introduced as a rapturous finale to this iteration of *Paradise Lost*, this festive scene testifies to a return of the life-enhancing energies of the Dionysiac last seen so exuberantly in *Garden of Earthly Delights*. Relatedly, Shaw produced two works inspired by a fresco by Annibale Carracci that portrays Dionysus returning from the conquest of India in a chariot pulled by two tigers with an entourage of libidinous satyrs and wildly dancing maenads.[33] The peacock-headed dancers and musicians appear in the variations on this picture. Color attains a dazzling radiance in the final section of the painting. A rhythmic sequence of bright vermillion Japanese umbrellas "dance" across the contrasting green of vegetation contributing to the

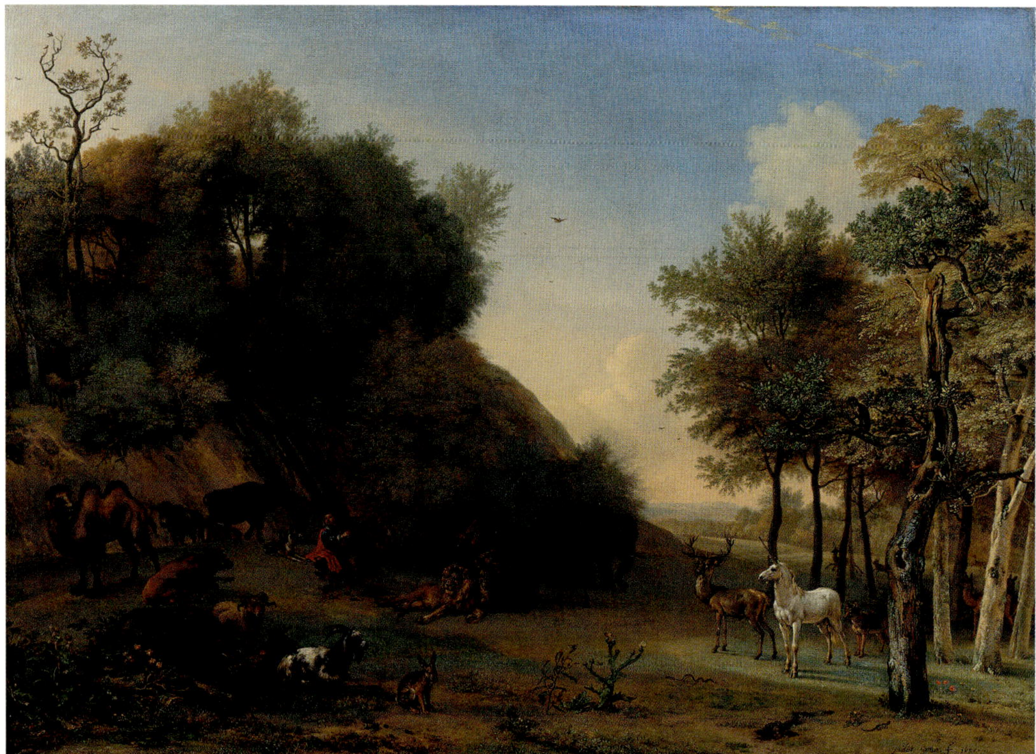

13 Paulus Potter (Dutch, 1625–1654). *Orpheus and the Animals*, 1650. Oil on canvas; 67 × 89 cm (26¼ × 35 in.). Rijksmuseum, Amsterdam.

festive air. In the aforementioned works that reference Carracci's procession of Dionysus, Shaw alluded to Shiva, the Hindu god of dance, shown in devotional statues balanced on one leg. Syncretism, a fundamental principle of Shaw's oeuvre, results in a three-way identification of Dionysus, Shiva, and Shaw himself. Drawing together myths and motifs from Asia and the West, syncretism counters the separation that is the inevitable corollary of exile, reassembling from the Babel of disparate languages, cultures, and religions a lost primordial unity.[34]

A peacock-headed man with a lyre perched in the foreground at the far right is the god Orpheus (see p. 54), famed in Greek myth for his ability to charm trees, wild animals, and even rocks with his playing. Draped loosely about this imposing figure is the trademark Kashmiri shawl, identifying him as another avatar of Shaw. In Hindu mythology, Krishna is sometimes represented as a herdsman playing a flute with the cows sacred to him gathered round, a subject that Shaw has painted as a one-off commission (*Lord Krishna*, 2019; Usha Mittal Collection).[35] Orpheus enchanting the animals is a popular theme in Golden Age Dutch art. It is a variation on the Garden of Eden where Adam and Eve are surrounded by all the animals of the Creation but without the connotations of dominion over nature and with only a single figure. Both subjects grew in popularity as animals brought back from the New World were seen by European artists for the first time. The unicorn is a surprise inclusion in Paulus Potter's *Orpheus and the Animals* and Cranach's *Garden of Eden* (fig. 13), since to our eyes it is a purely fictional beast, yet Pliny the Elder, whose *Natural History* remained influential in Renaissance Europe, contended they were real and, moreover, were to be found living in India.[36] It is wholly in keeping with such wisdom and iconographic precedent that Shaw has chosen to depict a unicorn at the right edge of *Paradise Lost*.[37]

Fraternity with animals is a constant of Shaw's paradisical vision.[38] They appear in his painting not singly but in great profusion: shoals, swarms, flocks, and herds of them. Peacocks with iridescent blue and green coloring and long trains like ceremonial robes appear in *Paradise Lost* twice before being adopted as a new hybrid personification. A magnificent jeweled peacock throne was a symbol of the extravagant reign of Mughal emperor Shah Jahan, famed for the Taj Mahal, whose kingdom promoted itself as an earthly paradise. No doubt Aesop's fable "A Peacock and a Crane," a cautionary tale about the peacock's showiness is familiar to Shaw:

> As a *Peacock* and a *Crane* were in Company together, the *Peacock* spreads his Tail, and Challenges the Other, to shew him such a Fan of Feathers. The *Crane,* upon This, Springs up into the Air, and calls to the *Peacock* to Follow him if he could. You Brag of your Plumes, says he, that are Fair indeed to the Eye, but no way Useful or Fit for any manner of Service.[39]

Another curious case that mirrors Shaw's own exile are flocks of raucous green parakeets that appear in the final chapter of *Paradise Lost* (see p. 54) and several other pictures. First spotted in Kew Gardens, they have since gained a foothold across London's green spaces and occasionally touch down in Shaw's garden. They originate from sub-Saharan Africa and South Asia, where their habitat extends to the Himalayan foothills. One urban myth regarding them is that in 1968 Jimi Hendrix released a pair of the parakeets named Adam and Eve that went forth and multiplied.[40]

Discussion of paradise would be incomplete without mention of gardening to which Shaw has lately devoted whatever spare time painting leaves him. The paradisical garden at his own residence in Peckham, and the garden he has been working on for the past two years at Alderbrook, are creative expressions in their own right. Gardening parallels and complements his painting. While the one is a mournful elegy for a paradise lost, the other represents, in a sense, paradise regained. The garden as subject is reflected in such picture titles as *Agony in the Garden* and *A Summer of Sombre Stirrings in the Garden of Blissful Solitude*, and it appears as a setting in more besides. Inevitably, one thinks of Monet's garden and lily pond at Giverny, a universe in microcosm that from the 1890s becomes an inexhaustible source of motifs for his painting.[41] One suspects that Shaw would not have undertaken the *Four Seasons* series without a vivid awareness of changes wrought by the seasons in his own garden.[42] The right-hand section of *Paradise Lost* segues from Himalayan forest into a cultivated English garden, stocked with foxgloves, hollyhocks, daffodils, hydrangeas, tulips, and innumerable other plants, the perfect milieu for a paradisical luncheon on the grass.

This fourth section of *Paradise Lost* differs from *A Summer Odyssey* in one crucial respect: A pond covered with lotus flowers at the front of the picture is replaced by an impassable cliff face separating the viewer from paradise. A crouching figure of Narcissus no longer gazes at his own reflection on water but stares over the cliff edge into a bottomless abyss.[43] The presence of a unicorn, symbolizing the elusive goal of Shaw's quest, and the view across a verdant field to a fairy-tale tower, reinforces a sense of unreality. It is telling that Dante's *Divine Comedy*, which suggestively parallels Shaw's journey, contains meticulously detailed accounts of Hell and Purgatory, but when Dante reaches Paradise, he is blinded by the light and can only sketchily describe it. Dante is one of a roll call of writers and artists whose work arises out of, and is a powerful testament to, the experience of exile. Shaw has stated that *Paradise Lost*—his life's story, an unending search for a lost paradise—will only be finished with his own demise. It is *to be continued*.

NOTES

1 Dante Alighieri, *The Divine Comedy of Dante Alighieri: Paradiso*, trans. Allen Mandelbaum (University of California Press, 1982), https://danteonline.it/opere/index.php?opera=The%20Divine%20Comedy%20-%20tr.%20Mandelbaum.

2 The myth of the centaur is commonly explained as a misapprehension that arose when the Greeks encountered nomadic horsemen from the East and thought they were a single fused creature. See Alex Scobie, "The Origins of 'Centaurs,'" *Folklore* 89, no. 2 (1978): 142–47. Shaw's hybrid art is similarly born of a conceptual space spanning East and West. The epic *Mahabharata* describes beings similar to centaurs, the Kinnaras, who were half-man and half-horse.

3 The epic poem *Paradise Lost*, from which Shaw takes the title of his painting, narrates the Christian stories of creation and the fall of Adam and Eve. John Milton, *Paradise Lost*, bk. 1, line 756.

4 For an eye-opening insider account of the art market, see Orlando Whitfield, *All That Glitters: A Story of Friendship, Fraud, and Fine Art* (Profile Books, 2024).

5 Shaw greatly admires the Edwardian short story writer Saki (H. H. Munro), who employed animals for the purposes of caustic social satire. See "Books That Have Shaped Me" in this volume.

6 Milton, *Paradise Lost*, bk. 11, lines 750–52.

7 At the Glyndebourne Festival in 2016, Shaw exhibited three pictures that first included the pixies on swans in this section of the painting. For Ludwig, see Werner Bertram, *A Royal Recluse: Memories of Ludwig II of Bavaria* (Munich, 1900).

8 Raqib Shaw, WhatsApp message, Dec. 22, 2024.

9 The artificial grotto constructed by Ludwig was based in part on the Blue Grotto on the Isle of Capri. Rediscovered in 1826, Capri became a popular getaway for queer writers, artists, and photographers—a veritable Cytherea, or paradise.

10 *The Book of the Thousand Nights and One Night*, trans. John Payne, vol. 5 (London, 1882), 154–55.

11 This image is based on the poem "The Last Man" by Thomas Campbell, published in 1823. A spate of literary texts by Lord Byron, Mary Shelley, and others, before and after, explore this theme.

12 As an engineer, Martin was concerned about the inadequate sewers of the ever-expanding metropolis and came up with plans for reform that, however, were not adopted. See William Feaver, *The Art of John Martin* (Clarendon, 1975), 117.

13 Caspar David Friedrich, *Wanderer Above the Sea of Fog* (c. 1817), Hamburger Kunsthalle, Hamburg.

14 See Sabine Rewald, ed., *Caspar David Friedrich: Moonwatchers*, exh. cat. (Metropolitan Museum of Art, 2001).

15 Shaw, WhatsApp message, Dec. 22, 2024. The last phrase echoes the sentiments expressed by Dante in the epigraph to this chapter.

16 *Hermit* is Middle English and comes from the Old French *hermite*, from late Latin *eremita*, from Greek *erēmitēs*, from *erēmos*, meaning "solitary." A hermit cloaked in a Kashmiri shawl is foremost among the numerous masks or avatars—the latter a Sanskrit word—of the artist.

17 I am grateful to Madhuvanti Ghose for pointing out this connection to me. See Kazi K. Ashraf, *The Hermit's Hut: Architecture and Asceticism in India* (University of Hawai'i Press, 2015).

18 Shaw, WhatsApp message, Dec. 22, 2024.

19 Joris-Karl Huysmans, chap. 6 in *À Rebours*, trans. John Howard (Simon & Brown, 2018).

20 The listed works were made in 2022–23 as part of the *Space Between Dreams* series.

21 Des Esseintes also had the work of Odilon Redon on the walls of his monastic retreat.

22 Alan J. Berkowitz, *Patterns of Disengagement: The Practice and Portrayal of Reclusion in Early Medieval China* (Stanford University Press, 2000). Also instructive is Maja Lavrač's "On Parting, Separation and Longing in the Chinese Poetic Tradition," *Interlitteraria* 20, no. 2 (December 2015): 105–22.

23 Scroll paintings are unrolled on a table and viewed one section at a time. Shaw adapts the format to Western painting and its protocols of viewing.

24 *The Golden Legend, or Lives of the Saints*, comp. Jacobus de Voragine, trans. William Caxton, vol. 5 (Westminster, 1483), 94–98.

25 Saint Anthony's tribulations in the Egyptian desert are a favorite subject for visionary artists. Gustave Flaubert's novel *Temptation of Saint Anthony* (1874), which revels in Anthony's erotic torments, was the source for an infamous exercise in sacrilege by the Belgian artist Félicien Rops.

26 I visited Shaw's studio in Peckham, London, alone on Dec. 20, 2024, and on Jan. 21, 2025, with Madhuvanti Ghose. In the days after my first visit, Shaw and I exchanged WhatsApp messages, some of which are quoted elsewhere.

27 Milton, *Paradise Lost*, bk. 1, line 47.

28 Raqib Shaw, "Artists in Conversation: Raqib Shaw," interview by Rachel Stratton, Yale Center for British Art, February 28, 2025, video, 1 hr., https://britishart.yale.edu/exhibitions-programs/artists-conversation-raqib-shaw.

29 On the issue of religious iconoclasm, see Bruno Latour and Peter Weibel, eds., *Iconoclash: Beyond the Image Wars in Science, Religion and Art* (MIT Press, 2002).

30 Edward W. Said, *Reflections on Exile and Other Essays* (Granta, 2000), 186. See "Books That Have Shaped Me" in this volume.

31 Reindert L. Falkenburg, *Joachim Patinir: Landscape as an Image of the Pilgrimage of Life* (John Benjamins, 1988).

32 William Wordsworth, "I Wandered Lonely as a Cloud," 1807, Poetry Foundation, https://www.poetryfoundation.org/poems/45521/i-wandered-lonely-as-a-cloud.

33 Annibale Carracci, *Triumph of Bacchus and Ariadne* (1597), Farnese Gallery, Rome. Dionysus is the Greek god of wine, ecstasy, insanity, and theater. Bacchus is the equivalent god in Roman mythology. The two works by Shaw are *The Martyrdom of Icarus (After Honthorst and Carracci)* (2018; private collection) and *The Resurrection of Icarus* (2019–20; Samdani Art Foundation, Dhaka).

34 The hypothesis of a Proto-Indo-European language (PIE) proposes a common source for European and Indian languages, cultures, and myths. See J. P. Mallory and D. Q. Adams, *The Oxford Introduction to Proto-Indo-European and the Proto-Indo-European World* (Oxford University Press, 2006).

35 Apropos of Krishna as an Indian Orpheus, see Edouard Schuré, *Krishna and Orpheus: The Great Initiates of the East and West*, trans. F. Rothwell (Theosophical, 1904).

36 Ctesias (5th century BCE) wrote: "There are in India certain wild asses which are as large as horses, and larger. Their bodies are white, their heads dark red, and their eyes dark blue. They have a horn on the forehead which is about a foot and a half in length." Odell Shepard, *The Lore of the Unicorn* (George Allen & Unwin, 1930), 27. This claim is repeated verbatim in Medieval and Renaissance bestiaries. See, among others, Joannes Jonstonus, *Historiae Naturalis* (Amsterdam, 1657).

37 Shaw has indicated that the painting is unfinished; this will no longer be the right edge when the work is continued.

38 Absolutely key here is Friedrich Nietzsche's *Thus Spoke Zarathustra* (1883, repr. Penguin, 1974). See, in particular, chap. LVII, "The Convalescent," where Zarathustra takes refuge in a cave in the mountains, far above the rest of mankind, and is nursed by animals with whom he shares the doctrine of the eternal return.

39 Sir Roger L'Estrange, *Fables of Æsop and other eminent mythologists with morals and reflexions* (London, 1692), 204.

40 Nick Hunt, "The Great Green Expansion: How Ring-Necked Parakeets Took Over London," *Guardian*, Jun. 6, 2019.

41 See Octave Mirbeau, "Claude Monet et Giverny," *L'Art dans les deux mondes*, Mar. 7, 1891. "This man who could now aspire to all the vanities that fame affords its chosen ones, I love to see him, in the intervals between his work, in shirt sleeves, his hands blackened with earth, his face sun-dappled, happily sowing seeds in his garden, always dazzling with flowers." (My translation.) Mirbeau paints a vivid word picture of Monet's garden in each season as an ever-changing kaleidoscope of color, perfume, and botanical specimens.

42 *The Four Seasons* and *Times of the Day* are themes heavily linked with Romanticism. Philipp Otto Runge's *Die Tageszeiten* (*Times of Day*) engravings (1777–1810) are infused with vitalistic concepts of birth, growth, decay, and death.

43 For more on Shaw's exploration of Narcissus, see David Lomas, "Tears of Narcissus," in *Raqib Shaw: Paradise Lost*, ed. Honey Luard (White Cube, 2011), 43–52.

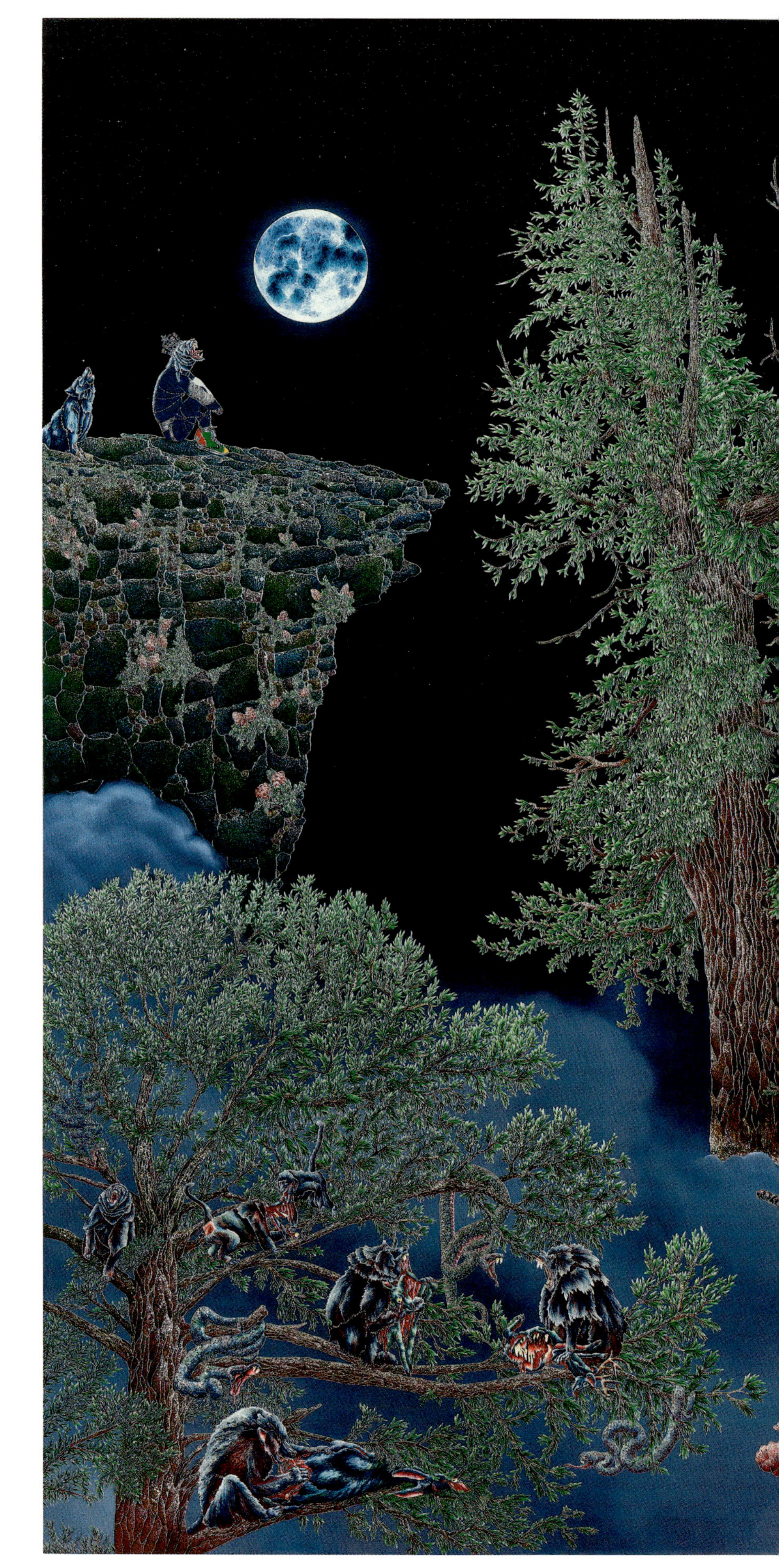

Raqib Shaw
Paradise Lost, 2009–25

Acrylic liner, acrylic paint, enamel, glitter, oil paint, and rhinestones on birchwood; 3 × 31.5 m (9 ft. 10⅛ in. × 103 ft. 4 in.). Collection of the artist.

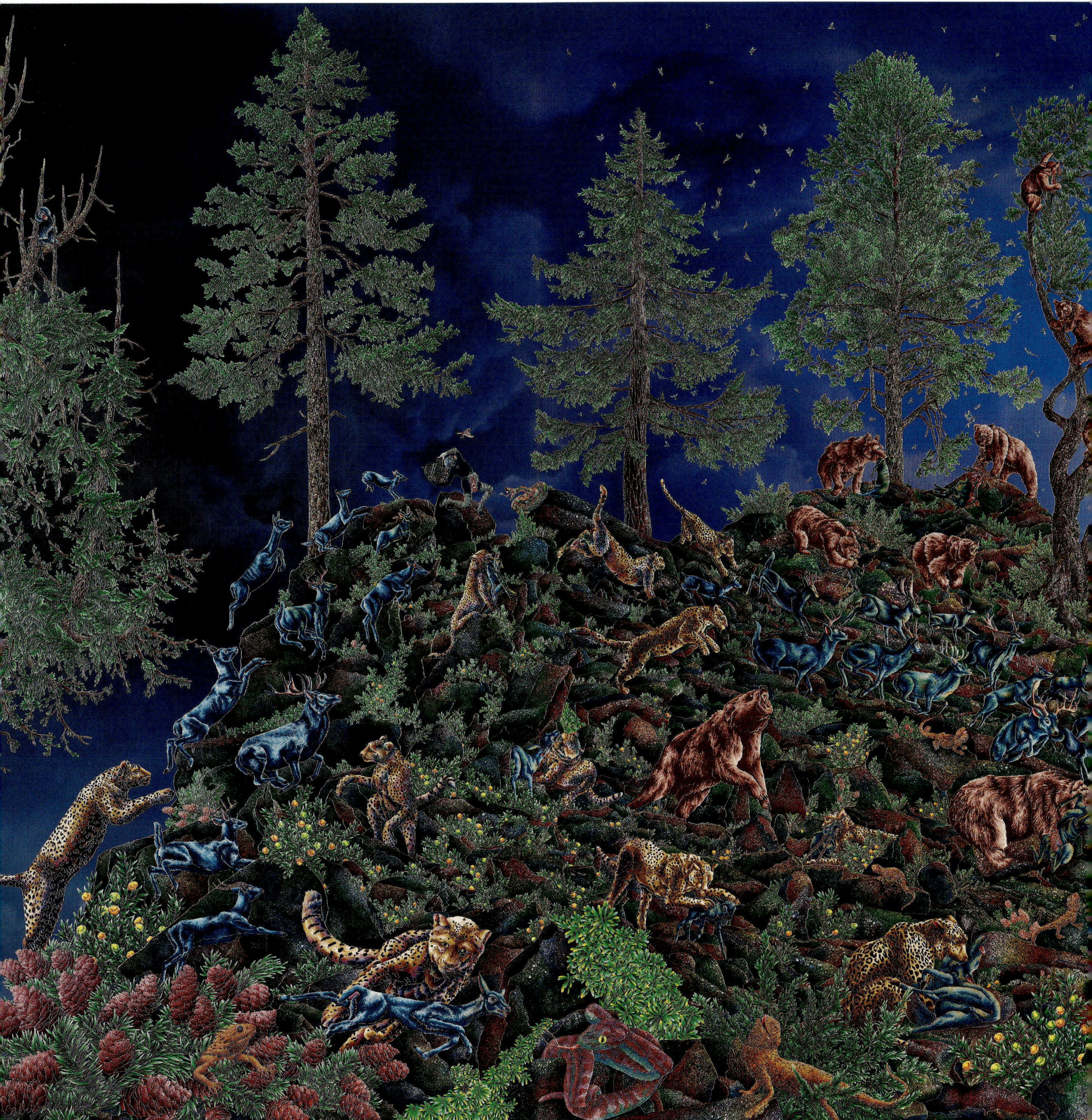

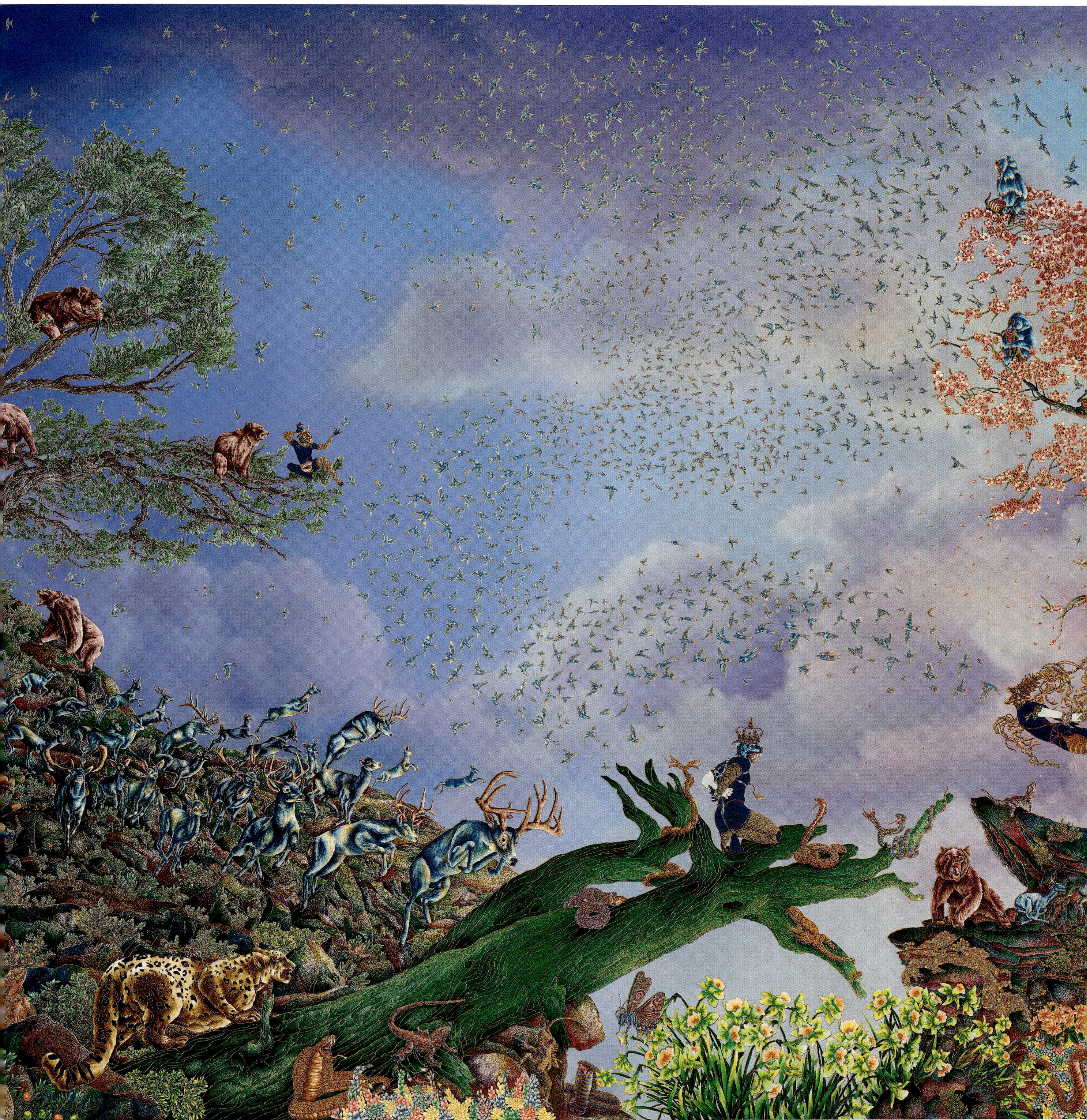

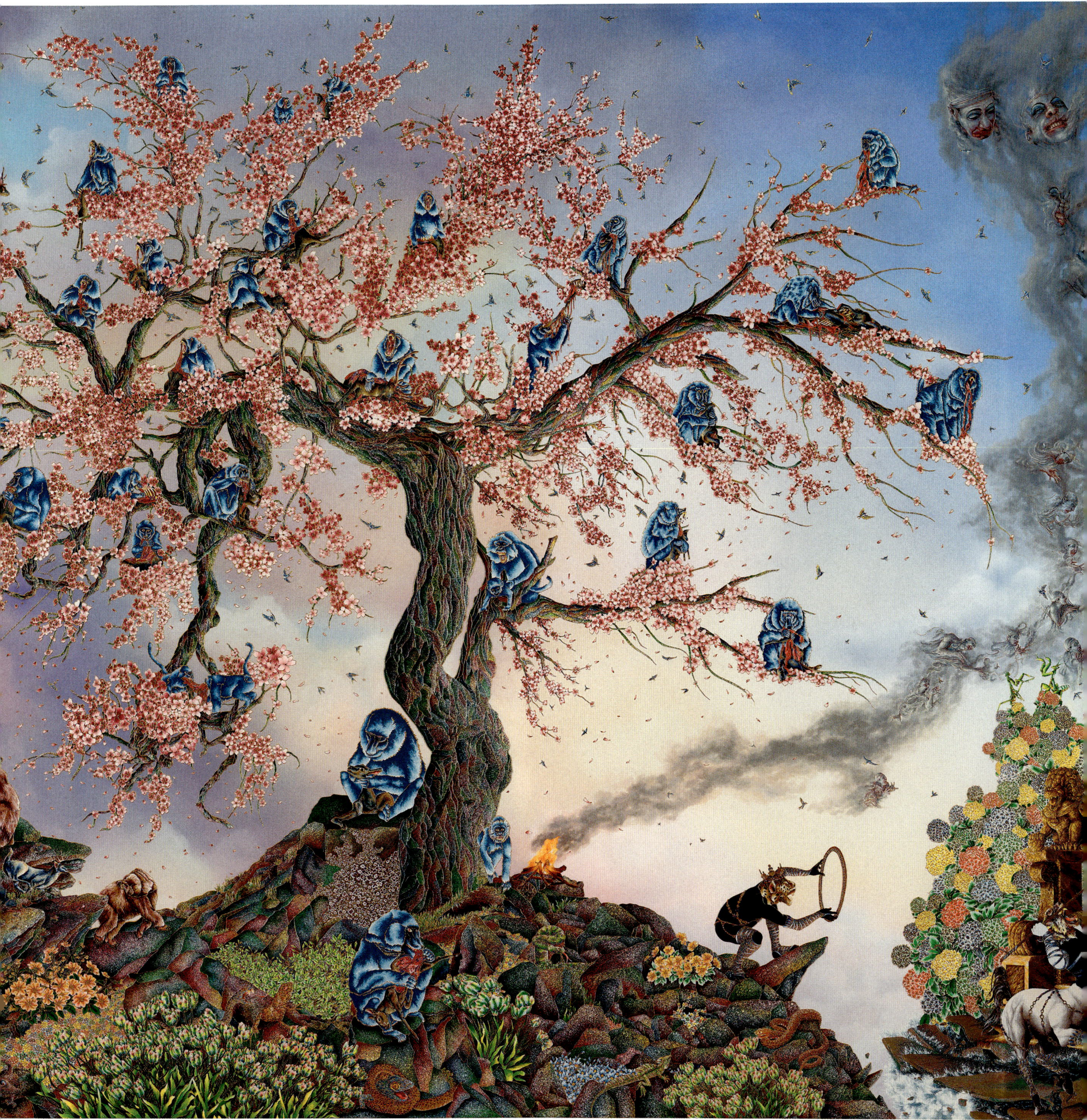

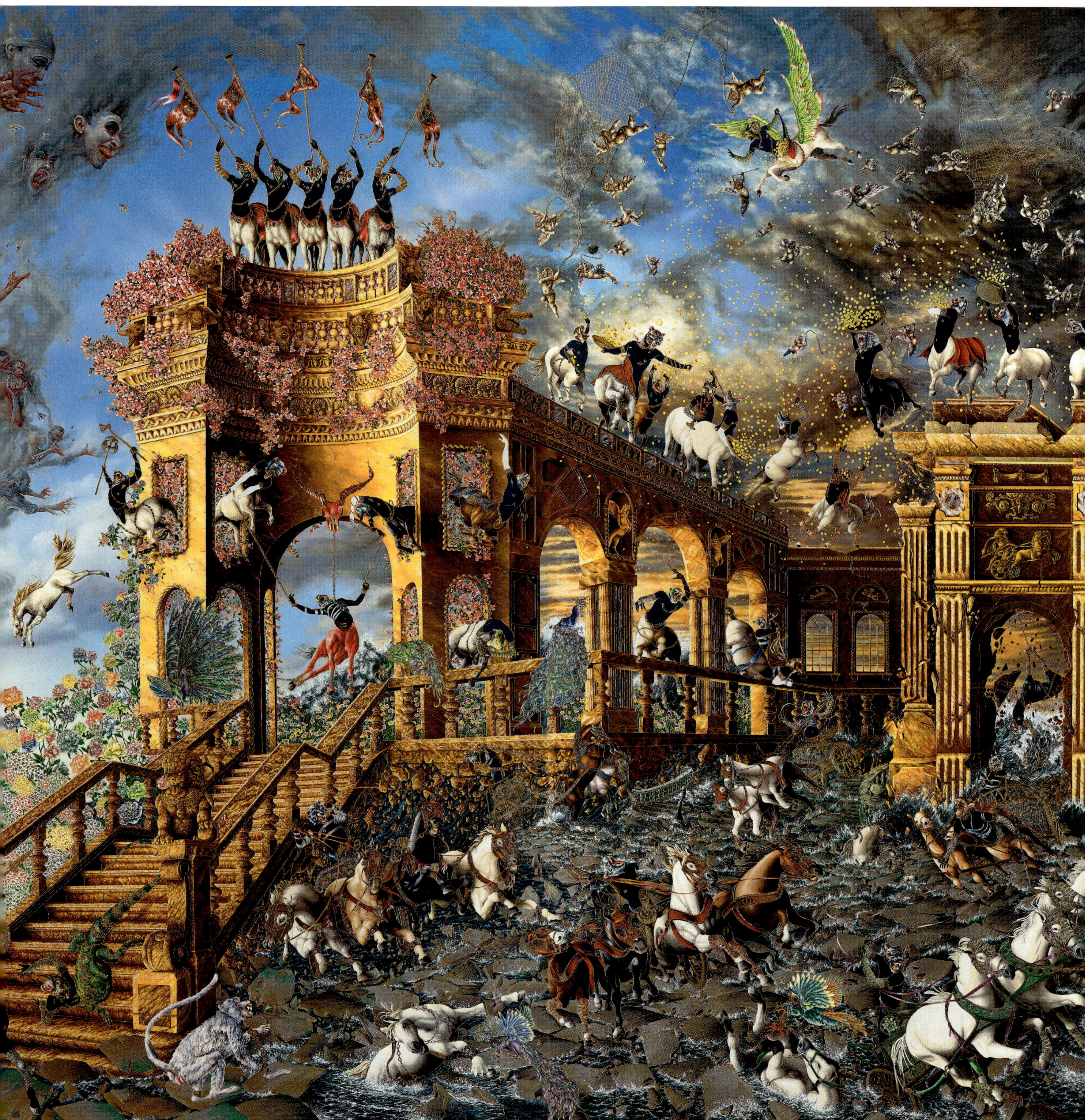

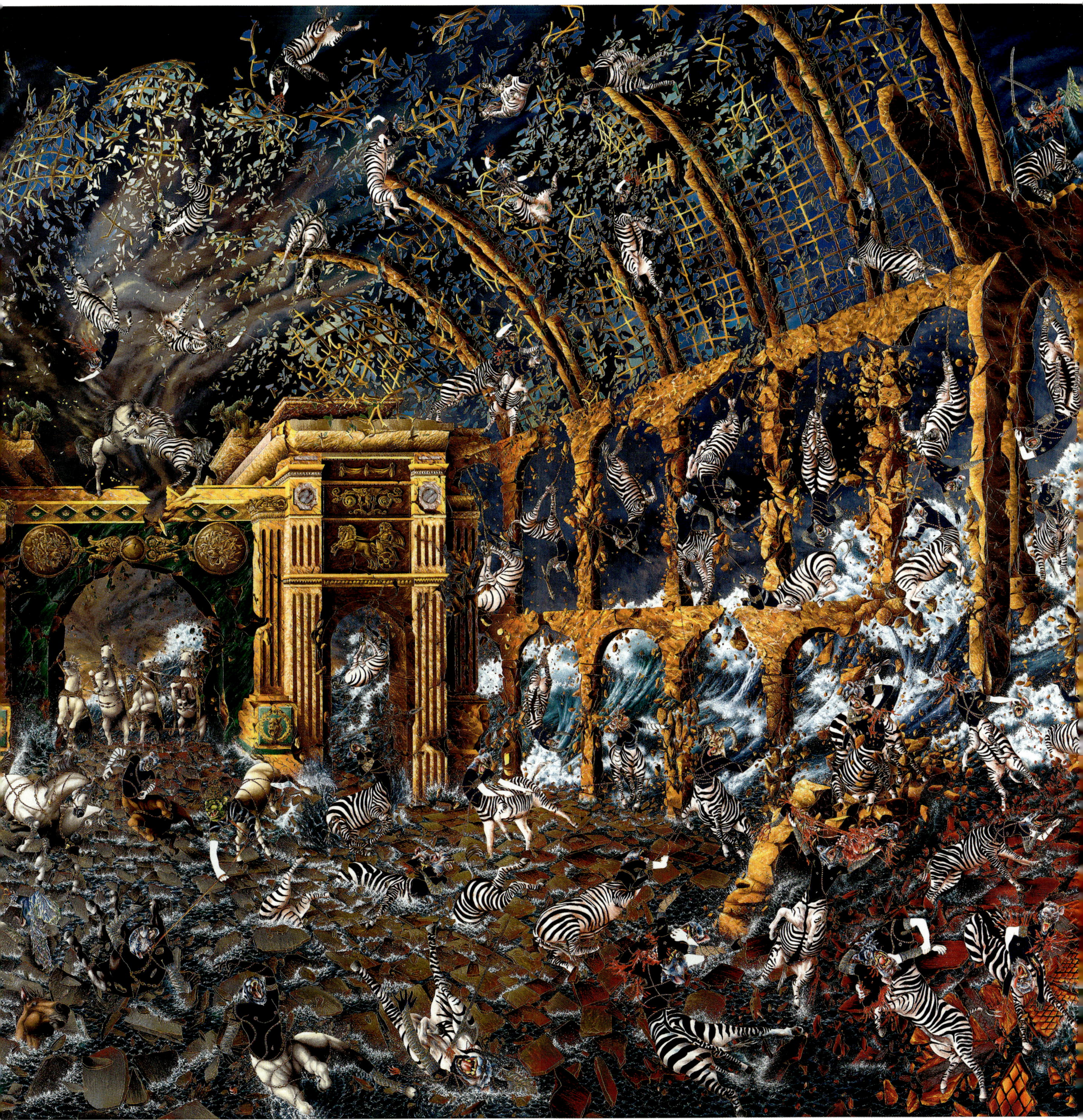

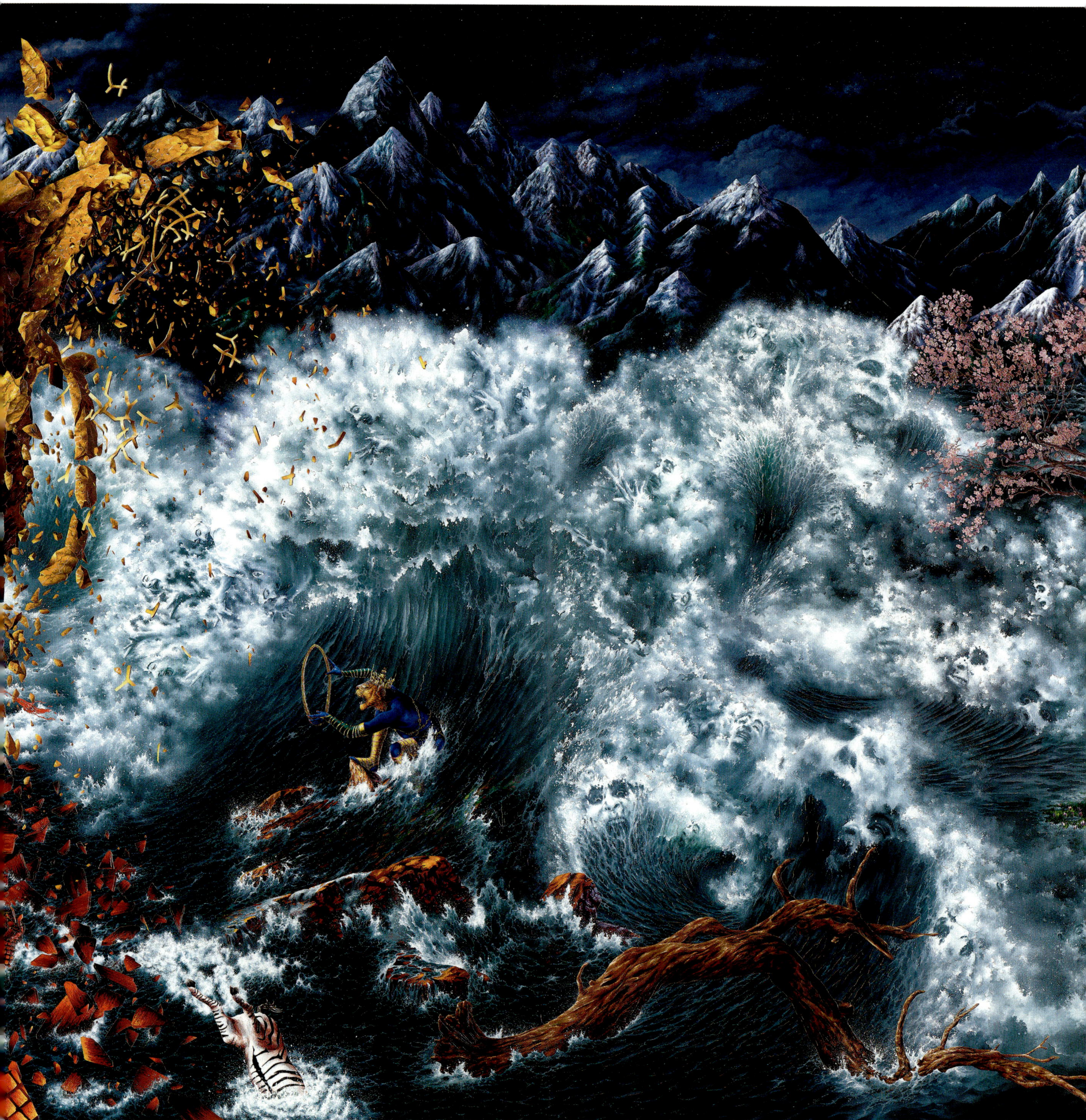

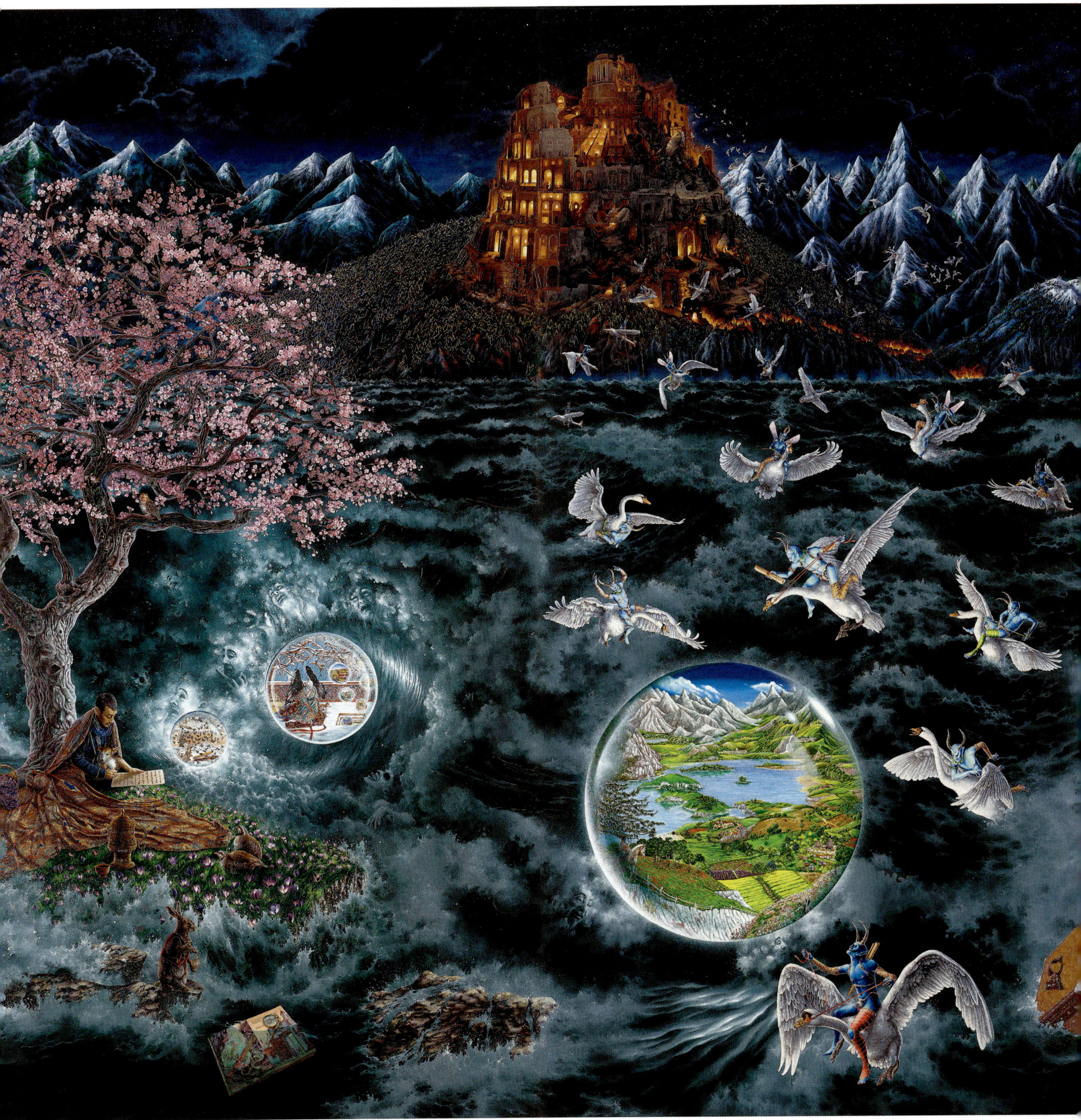

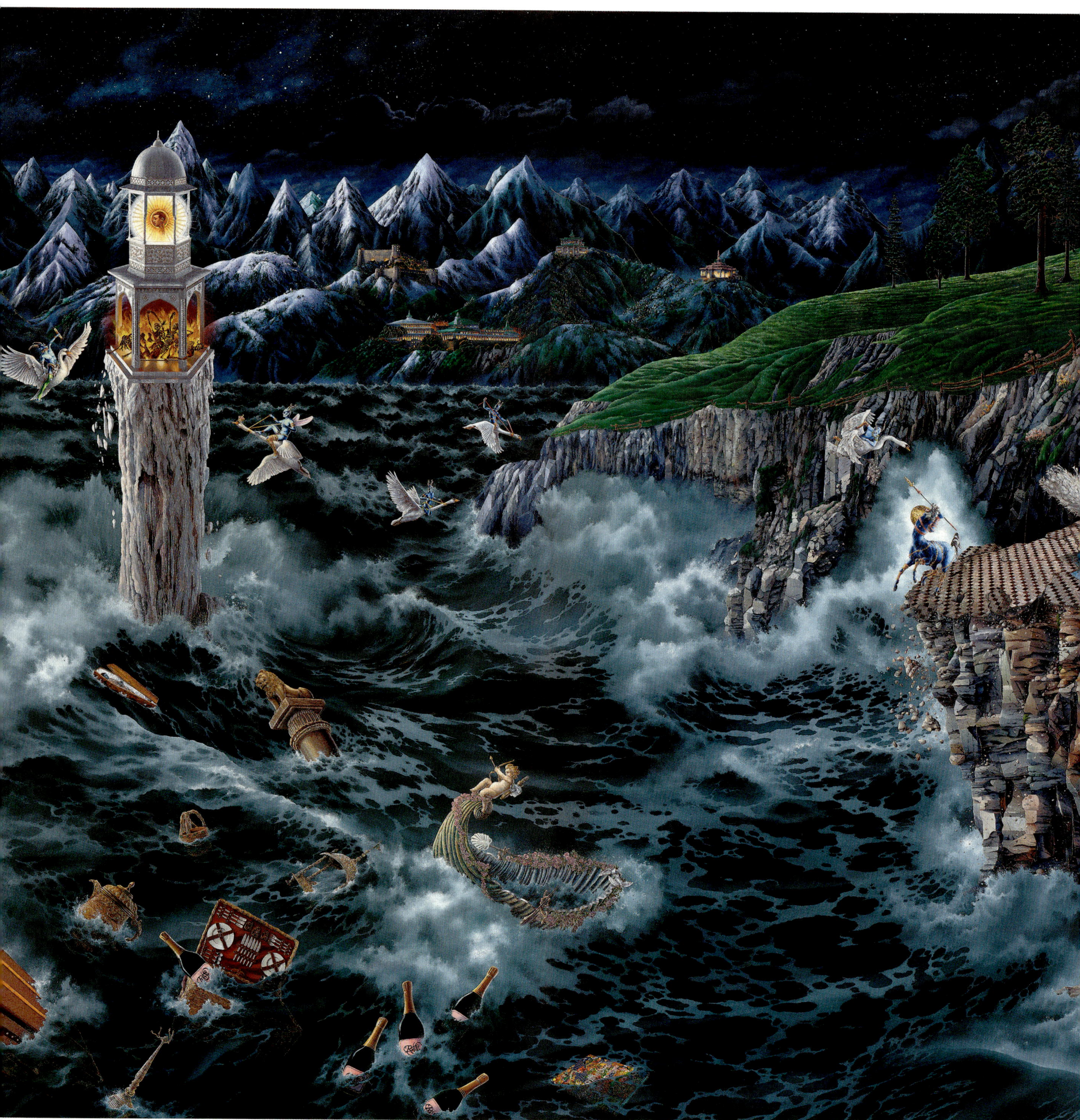

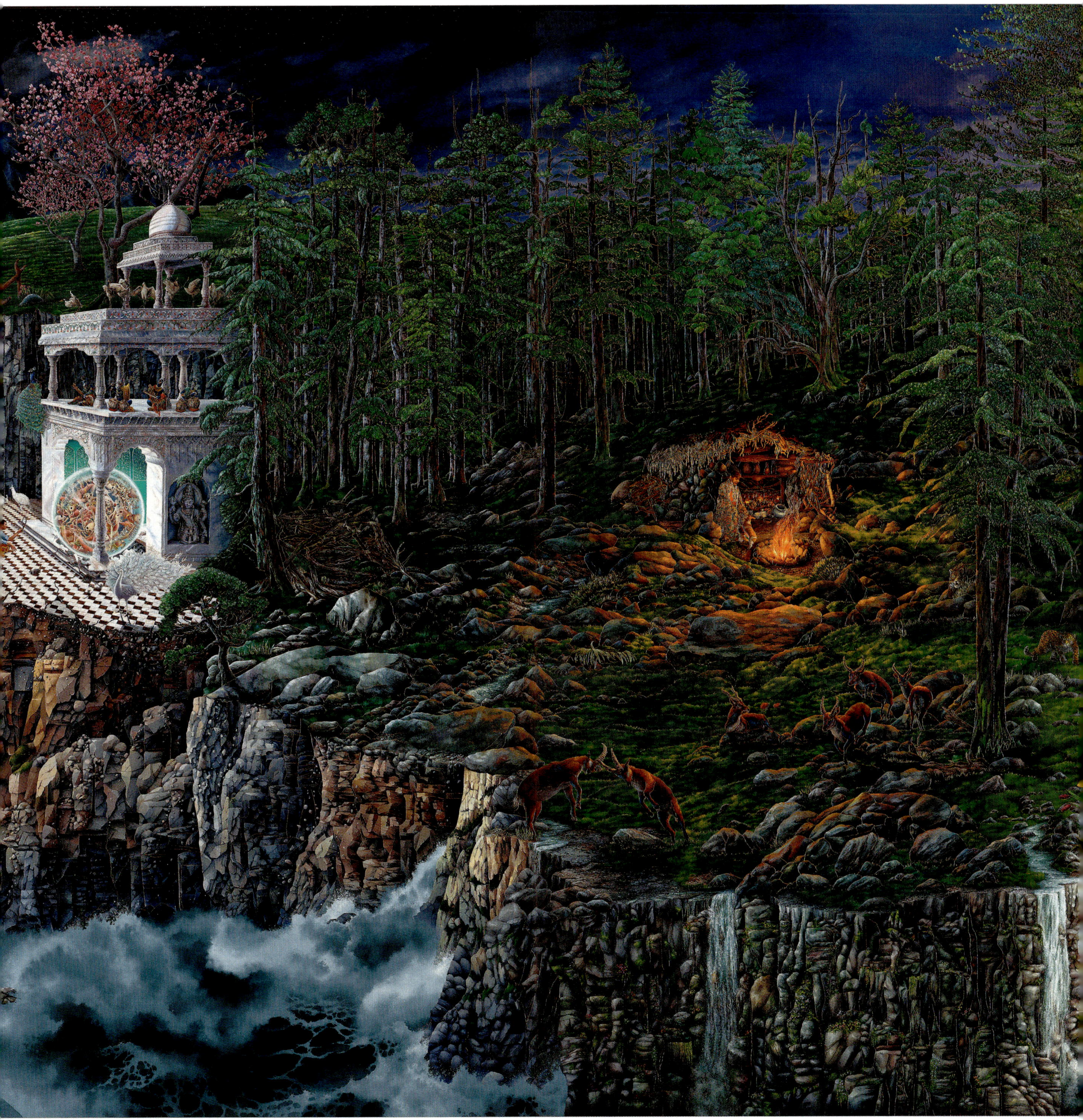

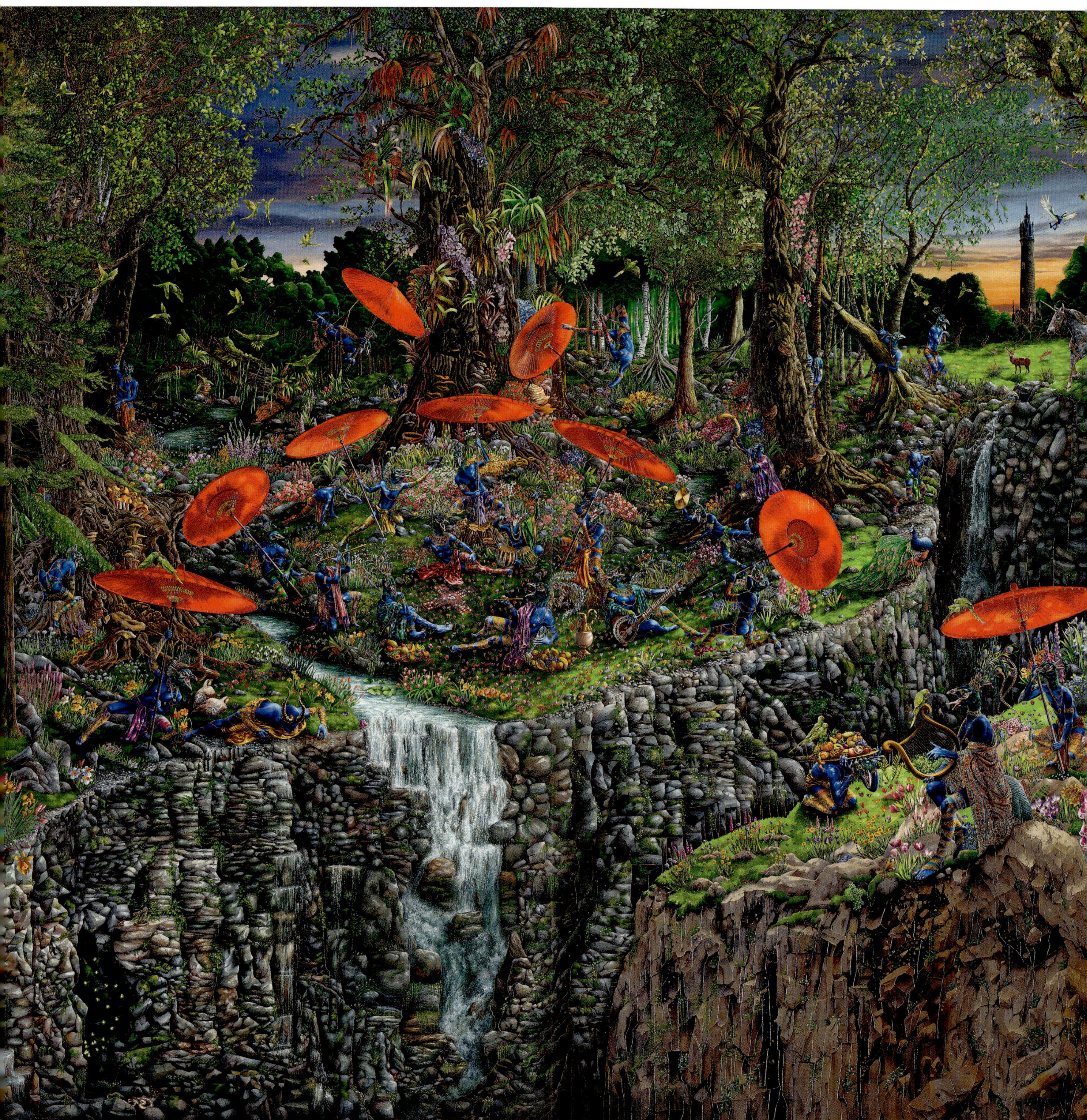

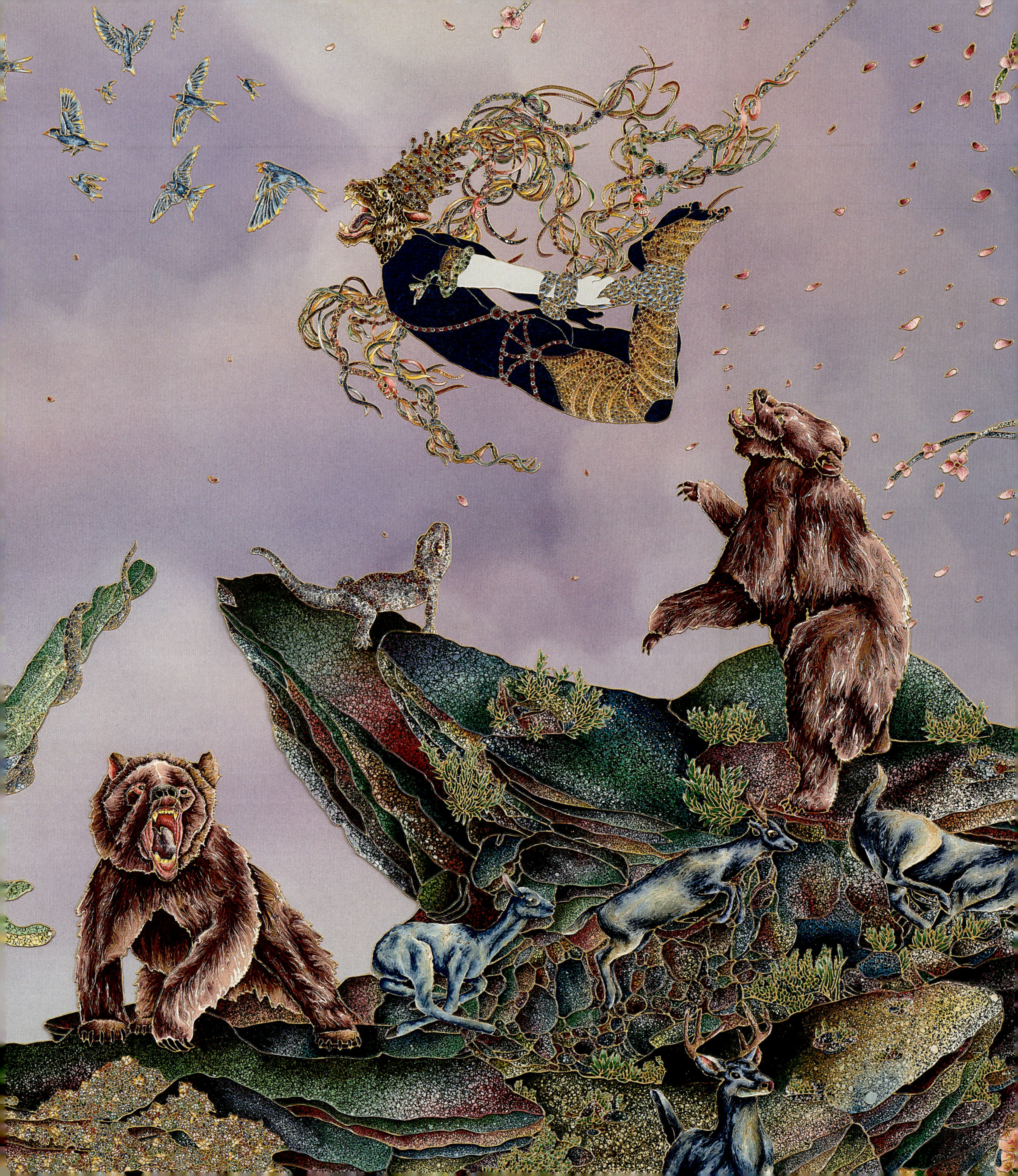

From *Jannat* to *Moksha*
The Illusory Worlds of Raqib Shaw

Madhuvanti Ghose

Raqib Shaw's painting *Paradise Lost* meditates—on a monumental scale—on the effects of absence and loss on an artist in exile. In the painting, which is inspired by Shaw's own life, he cast himself as a stand-in protagonist, painting the universal experiences of innocence, anticipation, anxiety, disappointment, loss, detachment, and contemplation.[1] "It is my own personal diary of my life, and it will end with my fears. . . . [It's] a parallel journey to the fall of man! . . . My journey . . . from youth to decrepitude and death and beyond."[2] Born in Calcutta, India, Shaw grew up in the Srinagar valley of Kashmir in an extended Muslim family. The family business dealt in antiquities, carpets, jewelry, and shawls. Shaw was exposed to an eclectic education; he attended a Christian school while being privately taught Hindu scriptures by Kashmiri pandit tutors.[3] Winters spent in Calcutta further opened his world to art and literature. The Western art historical references in Shaw's work are well-documented;[4] less known are his referents that draw upon his ecumenical upbringing and the visual culture of India and greater Asia. These global sources allow us to see the full picture of Shaw, a contemporary Kashmiri artist who has lived in self-exile in London for the last thirty years.

Jannat

Kashmir, Shaw's motherland, with its flowers, nature, poetry, and varied seasons, impacted his very soul. Shaw has repeatedly described the Kashmir of his childhood as an idyllic paradise.[5] The Kashmir Valley has for centuries excited the imaginations of artists and poets with its beauty. It has been described as *firdaus*, or *jannat*, literally paradise on earth.[6] A Persian couplet is often quoted to describe Kashmir: "agar firdaus bar roo–e zameen ast / hameen ast–o hameen ast–o hameen ast" (if there be paradise on earth, it is this, it is this, it is this).[7] When the Mughals first captured Kashmir in the sixteenth century, Emperor Jahangir (reigned 1605–27) regularly spent his summers there.[8] He was particularly entranced by its flora and fauna and directed his court artists to paint it.[9] Several local Kashmiri artists are known to have joined the imperial atelier.[10] The Mughals landscaped Kashmir, creating the gardens of Nishat Bagh and Shalimar (see fig. 1) gardens with orderly water channels, fountains, lush greenery, and flower beds gently rolling down in terraces to Dal Lake. They ordered nature in a quadrilateral *chahar bagh*, symbolizing the union of heaven and earth according to Islamic concepts of paradise.[11]

Buddhism flourished in Kashmir at least from the third century BCE, the time of the Mauryan emperor Ashoka. From Kashmir, Buddhism spread to Tibet, Central Asia, and China. For Hindus, Kashmir was also the seat of Shaivism; Vaishnavism flourished there as well. Kashmiri pandits also considered Sharada, the goddess of art, knowledge, learning, and music, particularly sacred. The valley gave refuge to Sufi sheikhs who helped Islam spread across the region (see fig. 2), and it was home to mystics and

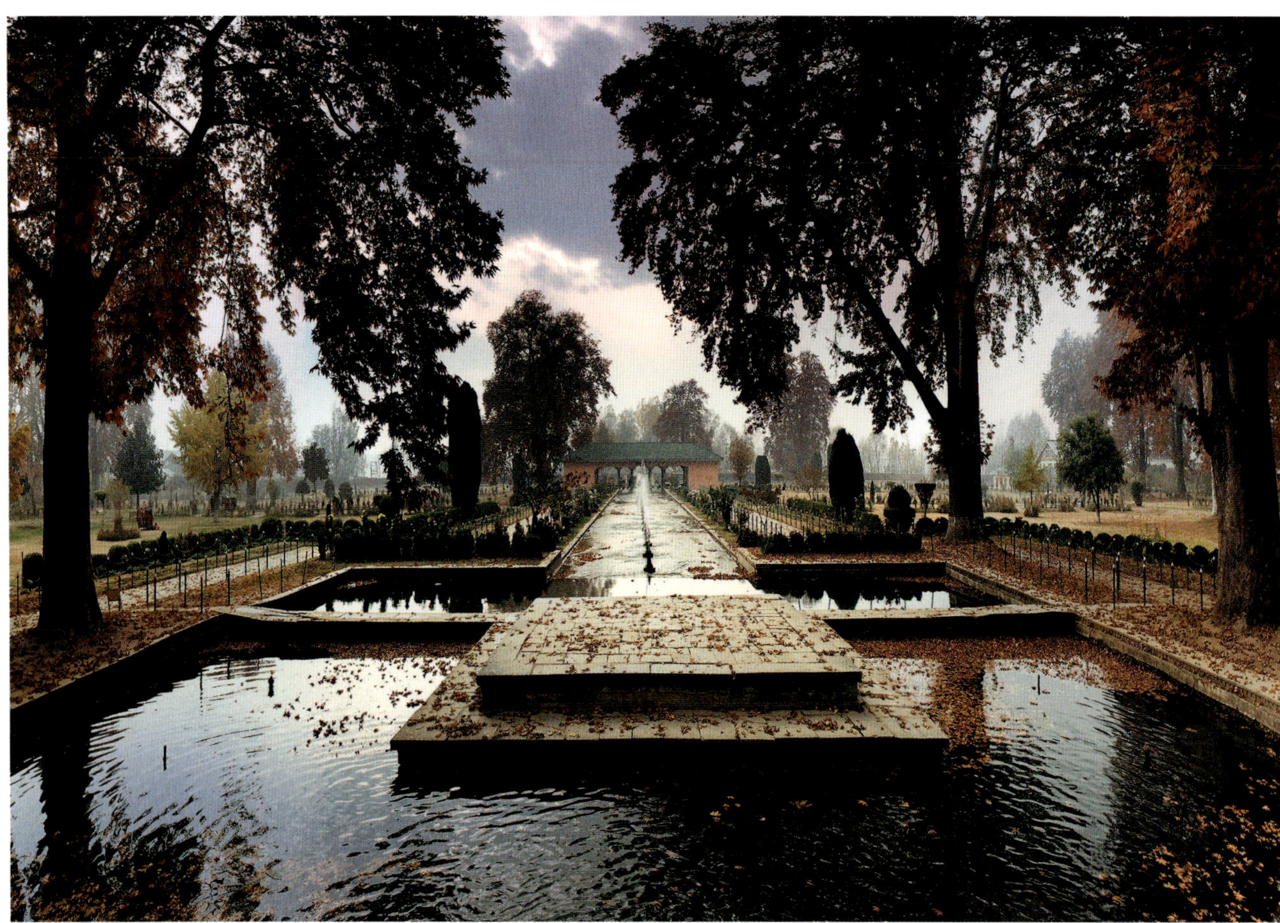

1 Shalimar Gardens, Srinagar, India.

saints such as Lal Ded and Nund Rishi.[12] The idea of *Kashmiriyat* (Kashmiriness)—that these diverse communities can live side-by-side in harmony—remains elusive in reality.[13] Despite its rich and multi-religious past, Kashmir's history has been one of perpetual war and strife.[14] Kashmir's ethereal beauty is a double-edged sword; along with its strategic location on trade routes, its beauty has made it a point of conflict between governments, resulting in four twentieth-century wars between neighboring India and Pakistan.[15] "Paradise" is today fissured by the Line of Control between India and Pakistan, with China also claiming a small slice.[16] Militant-led violence in the late 1980s forced the migration of Hindu pandits from the valley, and Kashmir is a Muslim majority region today.

The innocence of Shaw's childhood and the atmosphere of Kashmiriyat that he remembers were shattered by insurgency in the valley in 1989–90.[17] Kashmir had become too dangerous: In 1989 Shaw's family relocated from Srinagar to New Delhi, and Shaw himself has never returned.[18] Shaw's memories are clouded by his self-imposed exile from his motherland.[19] He remembers vividly a more peaceful time when the children of Muslim merchants could be tutored by Hindu pandits; such secularism has been lost by the generations growing up after the insurgency in a more polarized world. Shaw's voice as a Kashmiri artist in the diaspora is even more important in 2025 as Kashmir has plunged into another round of hostilities between nuclear-armed neighbors. He is among only a handful of Kashmiri artists who can speak to the harmony of the bygone era and to the anger and pain of displacement.

All That Glitters

Shaw's studio is reminiscent of the kind of painting ateliers the Mughal emperors might have run, with a bevy of assistants dedicated to the art at hand.[20] Over his career, Shaw has developed a painstaking and distinctive painting technique with the use of

2 Prince Visiting an Ascetic During a Hunt, c. 1625–50. Kashmir, India. Opaque watercolor, gold, and ink on paper; image: 26.5 × 15.2 cm (10⅜ × 6 in.). The Art Institute of Chicago, Kate S. Buckingham Endowment, 1995.267.

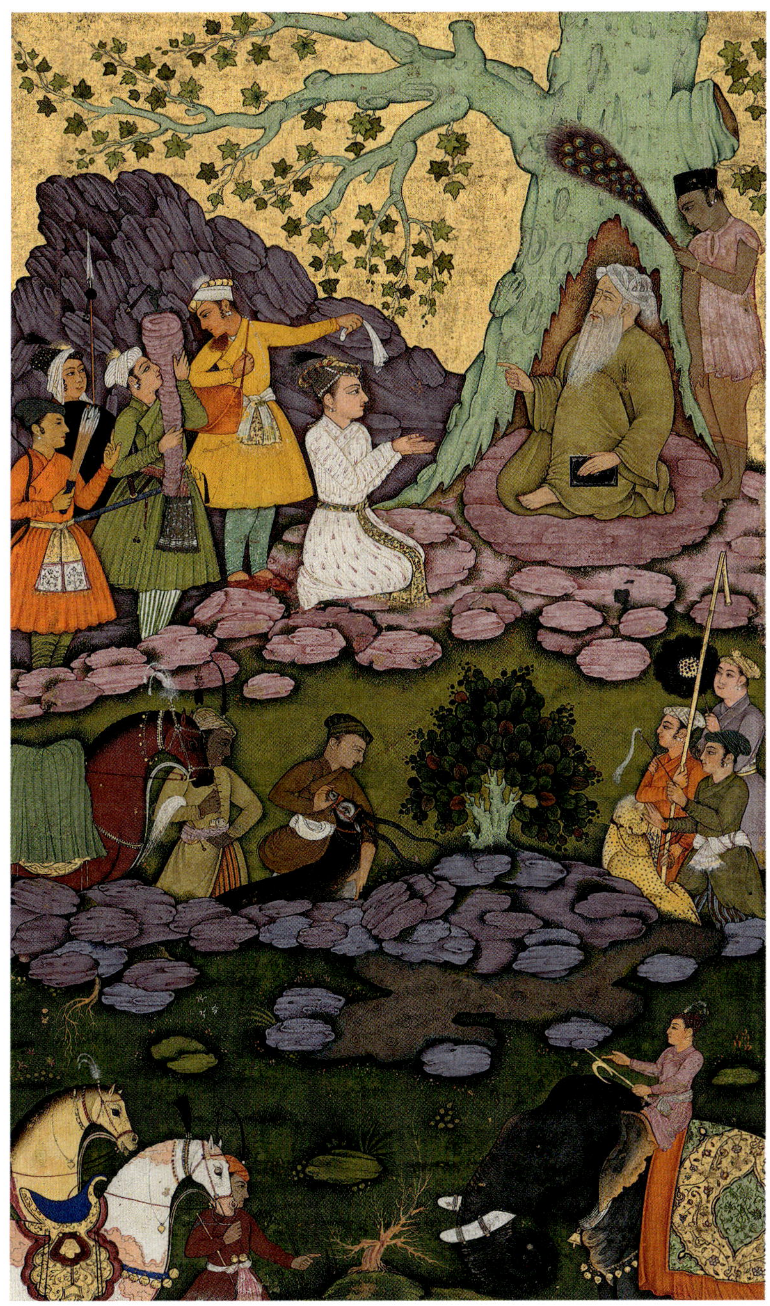

porcupine quills, which, like the squirrel-hair brushes used in traditional Indian miniature painting, require incredible patience and skill to master. The method results in elaborate detailing, as seen in the vivid rocks in the first section of *Paradise Lost* (see p. 47).[21] This patterning evokes the long tradition of Kashmiri papier-mâché. Artists employ this technique, which uses paper pulp waste, to create small, everyday items, such as pen cases. Papier-mâché also decorates the interiors (and sometimes the exteriors) of the mosques and Sufi shrines in the Srinagar valley, including the Shah Hamadan mosque (see fig. 3), which the young Shaw remembers visiting with his mother. "It was incredible to see everything covered," he has said. "There was no figuration . . . like much of the Islamic world, but Kashmir did have its own kind of color, which was of course inspired by the flora and fauna of the place. . . . In a way, this was my first introduction to so-called aesthetics."[22] Papier-mâché was brought along with other craft techniques to Kashmir in the fifteenth century from Central Asia under the patronage of the Kashmiri king Zain-ul-Abidin and has flourished ever since among descendants of the original artisans primarily within the region's Shi'a Muslim communities.[23] Today it is mainly employed to produce items for the tourist trade.

As Islam forbids the depiction of the human form, geometric and floral patterns predominate within Islamic artistic traditions and can be seen widely across Kashmir on the walls of mosques and Sufi holy shrines, as well as in the decorative arts for which the valley is renowned, from woodwork to embroidered shawls and chased metal objects (see fig. 4).[24] The richness of such ornamental design, all around in Kashmir, influenced Shaw as he grew up.

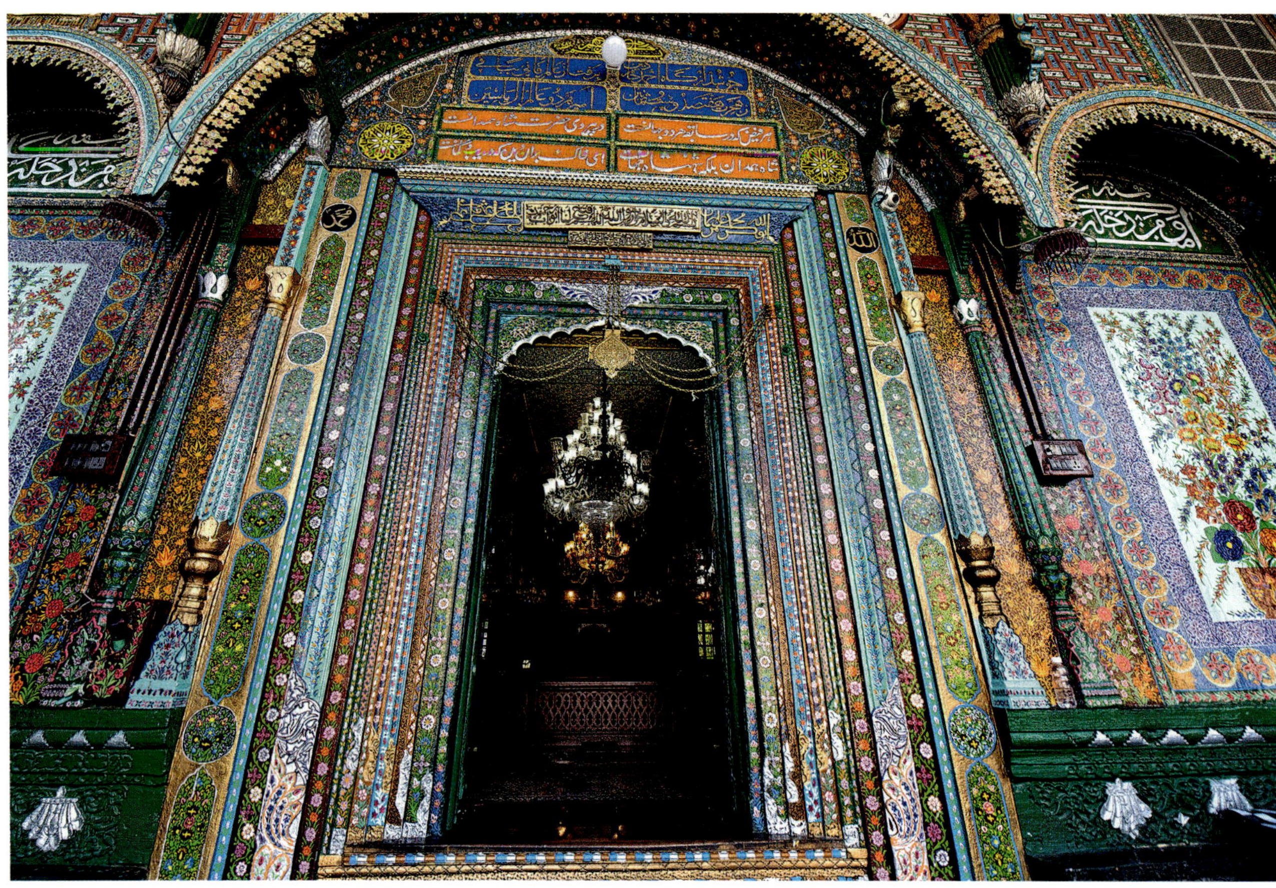

3 Shah Hamadan mosque, Srinagar, India.

4 Folding Qur'an Stand, late 19th century. Possibly Kashmir, India. Openwork gold-damascened steel in koftgari technique; 16 × 34 cm (6⁵⁄₁₆ × 13⅜ in.). The Art Institute of Chicago, Chicago Collectors Circle, Friends of Indian and Islamic Art, and Asian Art Council Acquisition funds, 2018.126.

5 Detail of *Paradise Lost* (see p. 45).

What little Kashmiri painting that did exist (fig. 2) was not readily available for people to see: Paintings were usually held in albums in personal libraries.[25] Shaw was accustomed to seeing art only in reproductions; he has described being transfixed by the figurative paintings he saw at the National Gallery when he first went to London as a teenager.[26]

In *Paradise Lost* and other works, Shaw took his ornamentation one step further, embellishing the surface of the painting with glitter and rhinestones (fig. 5). This style of insetting stones recalls the popular Indian *kundan* technique, wherein precious gems are inset upon enamel and used to make exquisite jewelry and decorative objects (see fig. 6). Shaw's work reflects these influences in both its visual resonances and in the way he has evolved his technique, building up one layer over the other. Just as the Sufi shrines of his childhood feature layers of colorful papier-mâché and detailed lattice work (*khatamband*), so Shaw superimposed different forms of decoration in *Paradise Lost*.[27]

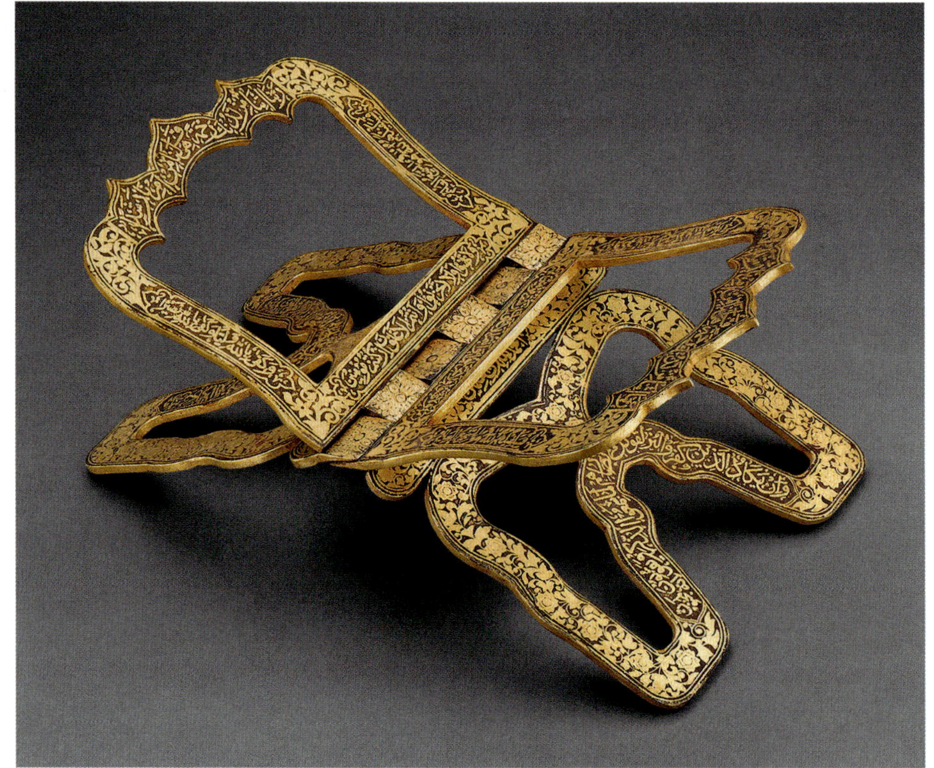

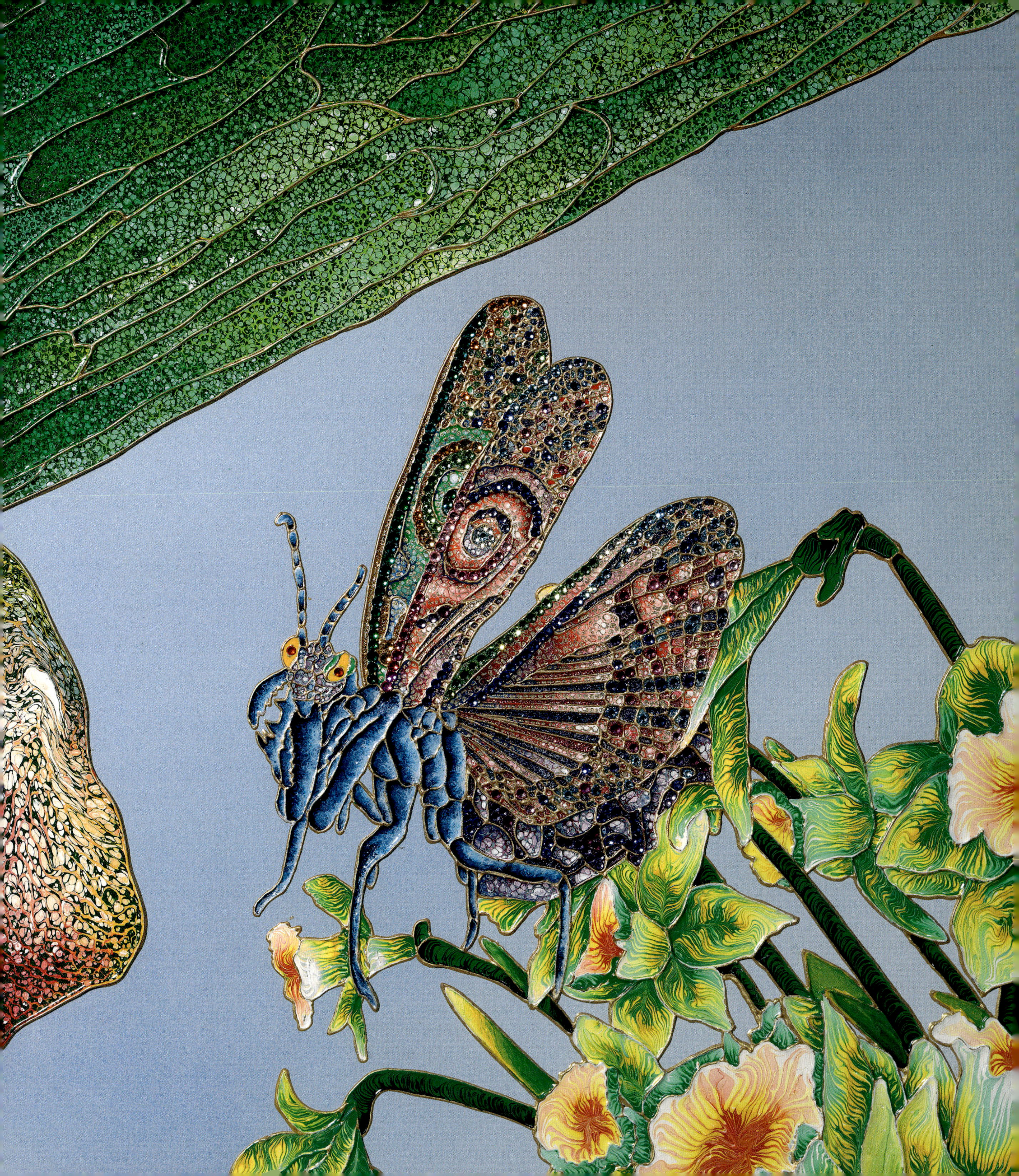

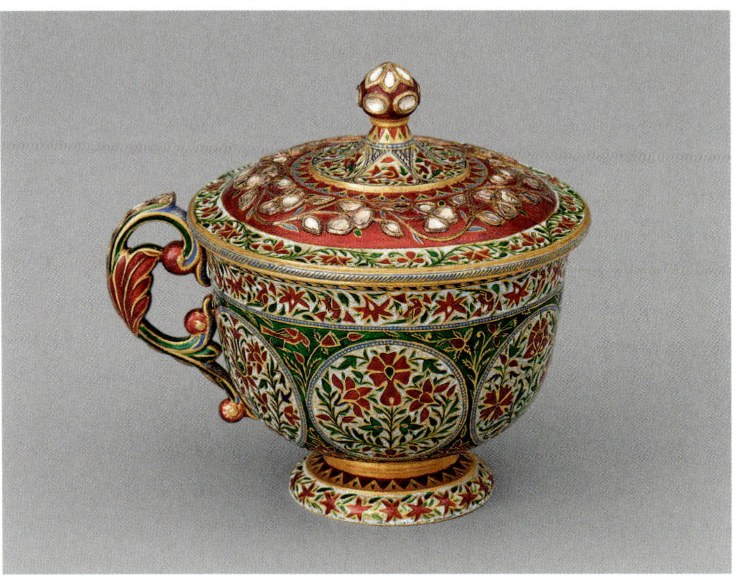

6 Wine Cup with Cover, 18th–19th century. Jaipur, Rajasthan, India. Gold and diamonds inset in the kundan technique with polychrome enamel; 9.2 × 11.6 × 9.3 cm (3⅝ × 4⅝ × 3⅝ in.). The Art Institute of Chicago, gift of Mr. and Mrs. Chester D. Tripp, 1967.541a–b.

The Artist as Avatar

Shaw portrayed himself at innumerable points throughout *Paradise Lost*—in straightforward self-portraits; as figures from Western mythology, including Icarus, Narcissus, and Orpheus; and as various animal-headed hybrids. The Hindu pantheon is full of hybrid creatures and gods with various animal heads; the many Indian festivals and the myths and legends associated with them enthralled Shaw from childhood. On the family's annual sojourn to Calcutta, Shaw encountered the autumnal Durga Puja festival with its many colorful characters, such as the buffalo-headed demon Mahishasura. Shaw also loved Indian comic books such as the Amar Chitra Katha series, which retells India's heroic tales for children and includes the monkey god Hanuman and elephant-headed god Ganesha. He watched the epics of the *Ramayana* and *Mahabharata* when they were first broadcast on television in 1987 and 1988—the whole of India would sit down to watch together.[28] The hybrid animals in this visual vocabulary became deeply embedded in Shaw's psyche. As he buried himself in India's vivid mythic past, he began to make sense of the world by imagining the people he encountered with animal heads or assigning them a certain beast.

He thought of himself in the same way. *Paradise Lost* begins with a humanoid creature with a leonine head sitting on a lonely cliff edge wearing a crown and colorful Dr. Martens and howling at the full moon, accompanied by a wolf (see p. 44).[29] Throughout the early section of *Paradise Lost*, this figure helps the viewer navigate from one section to another. On the rocky hilltop he opens a glittering birdcage to release the bird inside (see p. 45). The figure kneels on a fallen trunk and perches on a limb, in both instances oblivious of predators lying in wait (see p. 46).[30] Shaw signaled the creature's helplessness through bondage gear, tied hands, and kneeling posture. These avatars, each with a different animal's head, represent Shaw's vulnerability, his desire to escape, and his anticipation for the future.[31]

Shaw also painted himself as the young fawn being strangled by the baboon under the cherry "family tree" (see p. 47), reflecting his feelings of suffocation by his extended family and his fractured relationship with his mother.[32] He is also the curious chained monkey, visible at the bottom of the stairs, who gazes through his magnifying mirror in wonder at the flood-ravaged palace that represents the new world Shaw encountered in London (see p. 48). His circumstances—presumably as a penniless young artist—kept him in bondage to others. He is the preening peacock and the mythical, birdlike *simurgh* with brightly colored plumage trying to escape being trampled by the chariot at the bottom of the "kingdom of greed."[33] The simurgh frequently appears in Mughal and Kashmiri paintings.[34] Shaw stood out in his new world: Did he also see himself as the half-human, half-zebra creatures he calls zebrataurs? In 1621, Emperor Jahangir was given a zebra, an exotic

7 Ustad Mansur, known as Nadir al'Asr (active 1590–1624). *Emperor Jahangir's Zebra*, Mughal dynasty (1526–1857), 1621. Gouache on paper; 18.3 × 24.1 cm (7¼ × 9½ in.). Victoria & Albert Museum, London, IM23-1925.

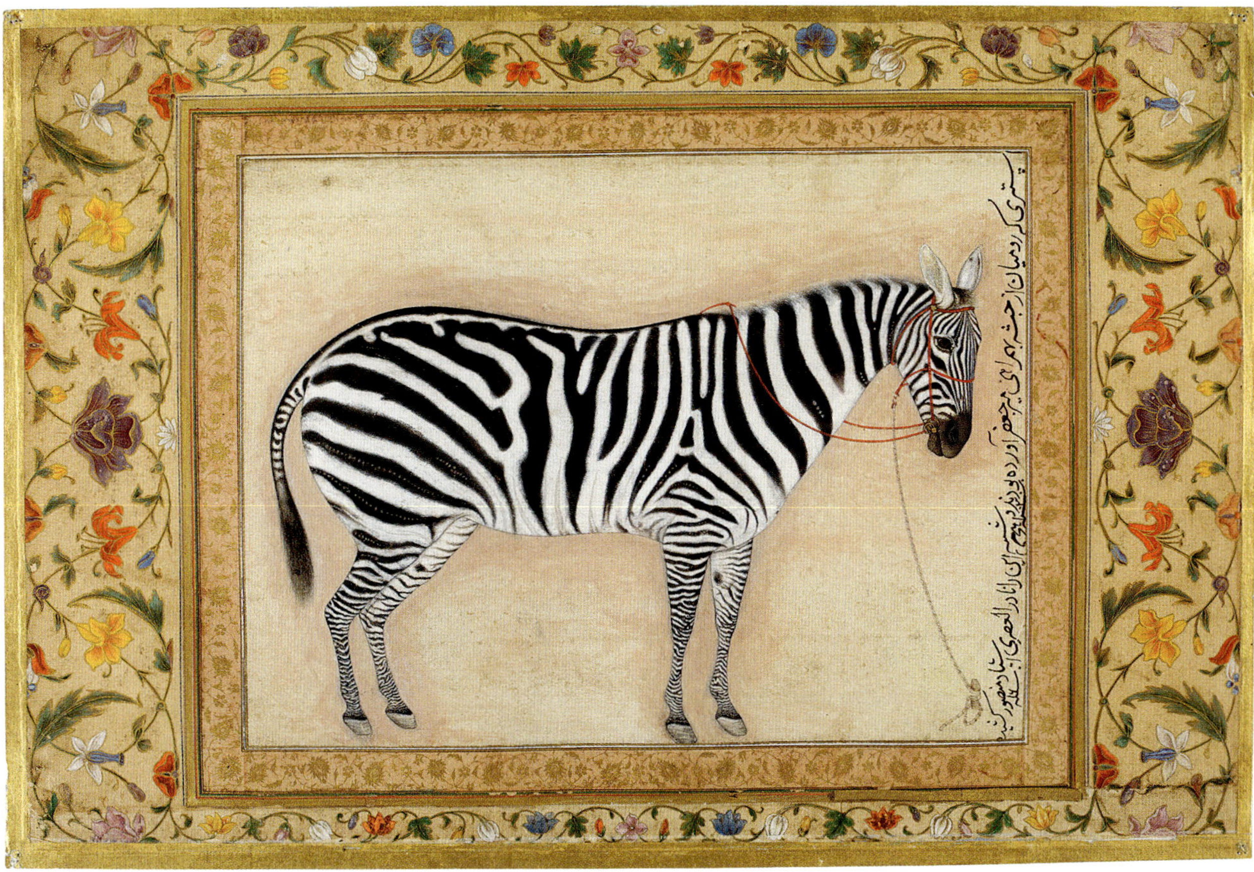

creature, which he had faithfully depicted by his favorite court artist, Mansur (fig. 7).[35] Was Shaw, like the zebra, one who would always stand out no matter how hard he might try to fit into a new environment?[36] Shaw has also created other animal-headed hybrids—leopard-headed centaurs and peacock-headed musicians with acrobatic attendants—and distinguished them into different tribes. The centaurs attack the zebrataurs, which are hung, drawn, and quartered or trying to escape the apocalypse.

Composite hybrid creatures have long been a feature of Mughal art, including that of Kashmir.[37] An Indian illustration from about 1700 (fig. 8), painted with a restrained color palette (*nim kalam*) depicts a harp-playing peri—similar to a fairy—in a howdah on a camel made up of European and Indian figures, some playing instruments.[38] In the camel's legs, larger animals disgorge smaller ones. This design—animals preying on each other—is often found in Mughal architectural and decorative arts, including carpet designs and carved ivory weapons. The jigsaw puzzle of interlocking humans and animals was a common artistic conceit.[39] Shaw grew up in a world of beautiful Kashmiri carpets and would have been familiar with such iconography.

Shaw also painted his face among the waves, in plumes of smoke, within tree trunks, and elsewhere, commenting on the scene like a Greek chorus. On either side of the painting's architectural centerpiece, Shaw included multiples of his face, each displaying a different emotion and stripped of the elaborate costuming found elsewhere.[40] These expressive

8 Angel (Peri) Riding a Composite Camel, c. 1700. Probably Deccan, India. Ink wash, gold and color on paper; image: 19.2 × 14.2 cm (7½ × 5⅝ in.); paper: 25 × 18.4 cm (9⅞ × 7¼ in.). The Art Institute of Chicago, Everett and Ann McNear Collection, 1981.219.

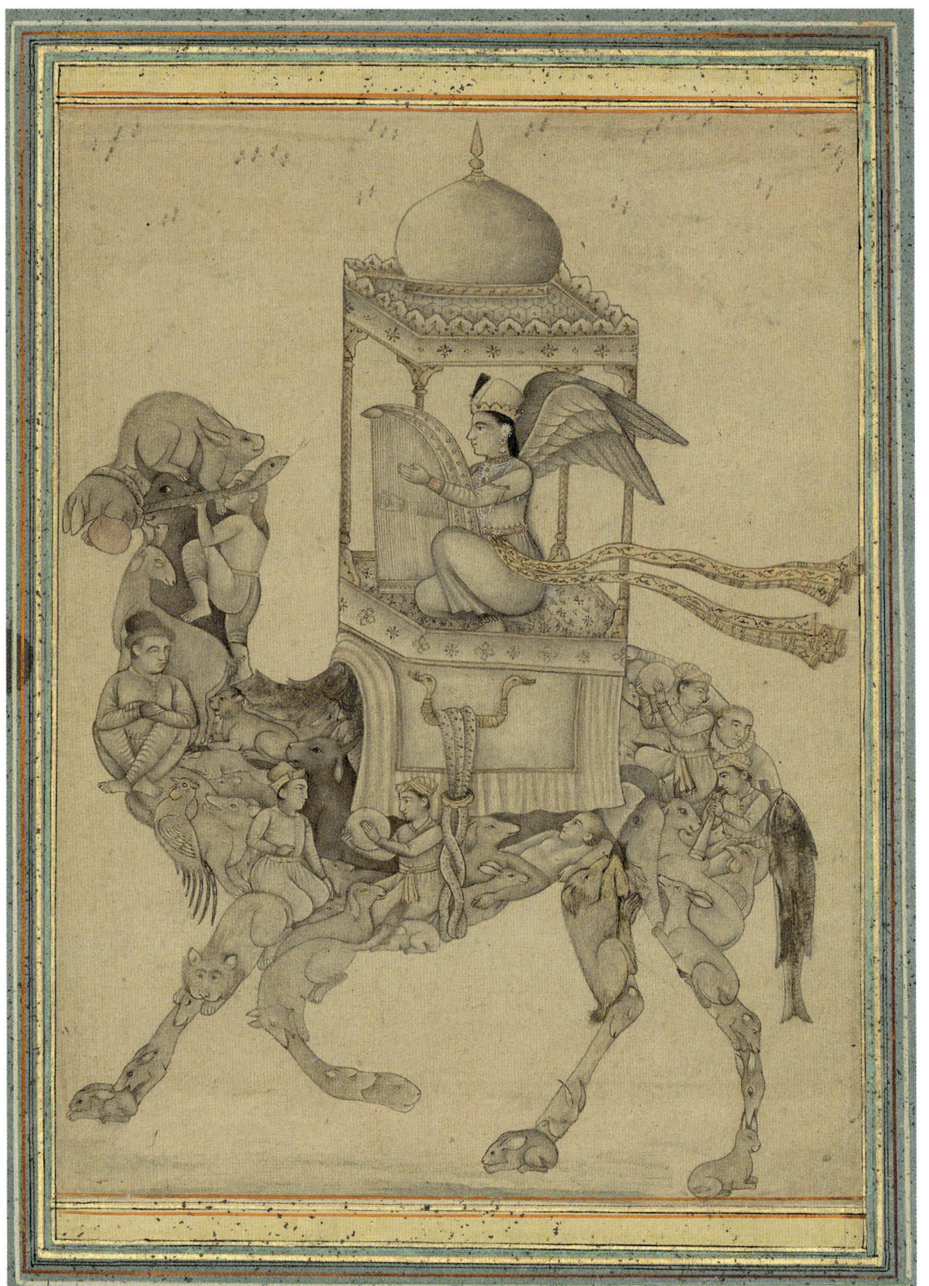

self-portraits encompass every type of *rasa*, or emotion, from pain (*dukha*) to laughter (*hasya*), and they self-consciously layer Shaw's emotions over the work (see fig. 9).

Moksha

There is a moment of tranquility at the center of *Paradise Lost*. We see Raqib Shaw unambiguously for the first time, sitting on an island (see p. 51).[41] This self-portrait is safe from the raging storm and surrounded by mementos of Kashmir. Framed by the high mountains of his homeland and sitting on a bed of native purple saffron (*Crocus sativus*), he is writing under another cherry tree, wrapped in his favorite Kashmiri shawl, an heirloom given to him by a close relative.[42] He holds his beloved Jack Russell terrier, Mr C, in his lap, and a pair of partridges sits quietly at his feet. At his side is a chased Kashmiri samovar for making *kahva* (tea). Into this quiet scene the artist has painted his own face in the tree trunk at the figure's back, revealing that the seated figure is still entangled in his memories. In fact, he is watching his memories float by as thought bubbles, each containing an important painting weighed down by meaning from his past: We see Kashmir with its bright mustard and poppy fields, glacial mountains, and icy lakes in the biggest bubble, while the artist, seated on a white horse, wrapped in his shawl with his dogs by his side looks on; in the distance, his previous home appears like a flashback.

Around the island of calm might be the flotsam of a shipwreck, but each object is steeped in meaning. The lion capital of the emperor Ashoka bobs by (see p. 52). There is a large trunk, a portable enameled

9 Raqib Shaw. Preparatory drawing for *Paradise Lost*, 2016.

10 Portable Domestic Hindu Shrine, c. 1880. Srinagar, India. Gilt copper and enamel; 89.5 × 35.6 × 35.6 cm (35¼ × 14 × 14 in.). Collection of Raqib Shaw.

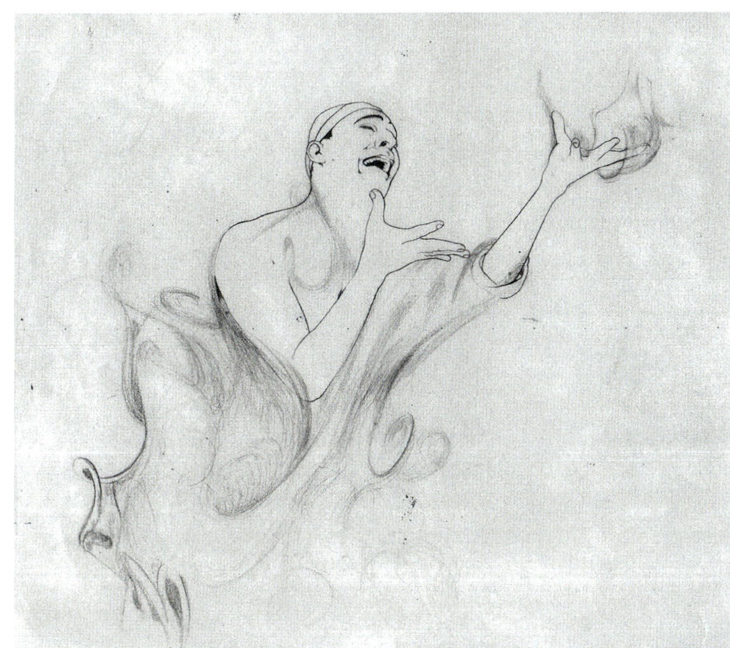

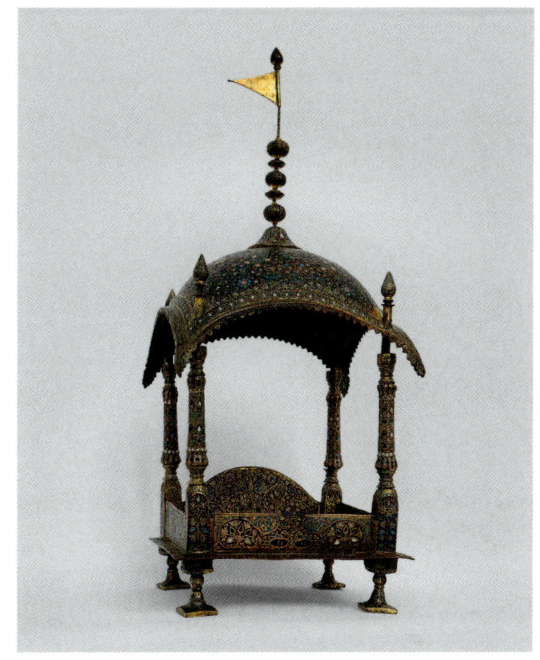

Hindu shrine (fig. 10), a silver rosewater sprinkler (*attardan*) to spray perfume in the air, and the samovar and basket that were just by his side. This is Shaw renouncing his ties to his homeland; the shrine, the attardan, and samovar have all featured in his paintings.[43] As he lets go of his past and his attachment to even his most precious possessions, the artist himself, blue-skinned and impeccably dressed, floats away in a coffin as he buries his ego.

Along with these symbols of home—and of Shaw—a Sotheby's auction catalogue with a record-breaking painting by Shaw on its cover washes away among bottles of champagne.[44] The painting's protagonist has given up these symbols of his heady past life, realizing that fame is transitory. A lighthouse emerges in the distance, its light emanating from the artist's haloed and severed portrait (see p. 52). Below, skeletons dance, mocking his success and revealing it to be hollow. The protagonist has realized that his memories of Kashmir can no longer provide the same succor that they once did.[45]

The crashing waves give way to a marble Indian palace like those Shaw would have seen on family holidays in Rajasthan.[46] We see the kimono-clad Shaw examining a thought bubble filled with skeletons through his looking glass (see pp. 52–53). They suggest that life is transient and that everything finally decays and dies.[47] The very cliff on which the edifice stands crumbles. But just beyond, in the depths of the forest, is a tiny, glowing fire. Here, the protagonist sits calmly in a crude shelter (see p. 53); there are no faces painted into the scenery. He has found true self-realization: *moksha*. In renouncing his memories of home and treasured possessions from his past, he has found refuge. He is hermit-like, at peace; he embraces the principle of nonattachment in his quest for enlightenment. This scene recalls a childhood lesson from Shaw's pandit teachers. In the ancient Hindu scripture, the *Bhagavad Gita*, the god Krishna tells the warrior Arjuna, as he is about to go to war against his own relatives, that the consequence of attachment is sorrow—one must learn to not be attached to things in life.[48]

In his search for enlightenment, Shaw has adopted as a personal mantra part of a fourteenth-century poem written by the Kashmiri mystic and poet Lal Ded, or Lalleshwari. These verses aptly describe Shaw's complete surrender to a higher force. Lal Ded was born into a learned Shaivite family but adopted Islam at a moment when Kashmir was in transition. The country had a succession of weak rulers as Islam was entering the valley.[49] Lal Ded's simple verses in the Kashmiri language are filled with metaphor and suffused with a fluidity between the different religious traditions that echoes Raqib Shaw's own upbringing and influences:

11 Detail of *Paradise Lost* (see p. 54).

The one who seals the singular sacred
syllable of "Omkar" clasped within the navel,
Hence carves the parting upon the head
of the cosmos without journey or travel.

With this one mantra engraved
upon the expanse of the soul,
A million other mantras flutter like
faded rags on a mountain pole.

I asked my guru a thousand times, what
is He called who has no name?
Exhausted body with wilting mind, I found
something from nothing in his game.

The guru gave me but one advice,
shun outside retreat within,
That replaced my prose and poetry,
for my naked dance to begin.

You have to endure lightning and cloud bursts,
live through stormy darkness at noon
You have to put yourself through the grinding
stone, starve yourself to a dry prune,

Jump in the fire, scare your ego out,
until you are nothing but an empty room,
Then close your eyes
and see with your heart, walls dissolving
to mountains under moon.

Seek your joy, soothe your pain in this paradise
garden, always laden with blooms will rise,
When your body lay bruised, your spirit
broken, in pain you close your eyes.[50]

Shaw has internalized these verses, relied on their message, and brought them to bear in his own life. This translation is his own, recorded from memory.

Maya

Just as he has combined Eastern and Western references within his work, Shaw is a product of both cultures. He has lived in London for over half his life, studying and now making a living there. But his paintings reveal a persistent longing for Kashmir. The final section of *Paradise Lost* entirely intermingles East and West (see p. 54). A group of peacock-headed men play *chaupar*, one of India's oldest games that is synonymous with a salutary lesson: In the epic poem the *Mahabharata*, Yudhisthira gambles away his entire kingdom and his family in several games of chaupar, which led to the Battle of Kurukshetra.[51] Flamboyant peacock-headed musicians play the sitar and tabla along with the flute and harp. Attendants go to extraordinary lengths to shade them with Japanese umbrellas.[52] But the artist did not set this idyllic scene in India.[53] Here, paradise is a glade in the English countryside. The overflowing bounty of summer is everywhere, shown by plates heaped high with fruit and by the surrounding rich vegetation and flowers, signifying wealth and plenitude.

But paradise cannot last, at least not in one of Shaw's paintings. Shaw painted this scene as a commentary on pre-Brexit society in England: what he viewed as a collective illusion. A chasm threatens beneath the rollicking peacock-men. Among them, Narcissus, a surrogate for the artist, looks for his reflection in the abyss (fig. 11). The scene recalls another nim kalam painting, an illustration of the fable of the

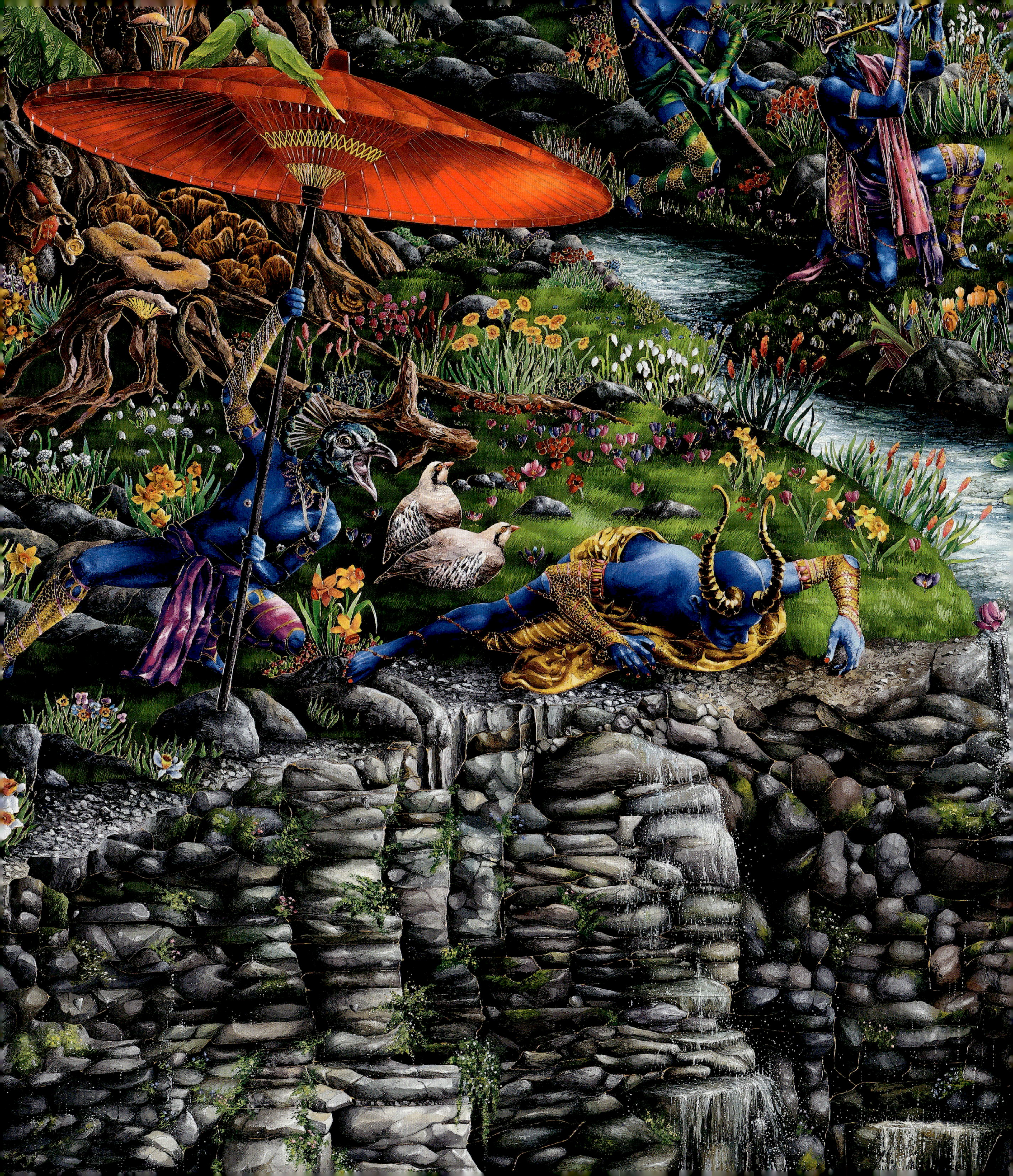

12 Attributed to Farrukh Chela (active 1580–1604), *The Greedy Dog*, Mughal dynasty (1526–1857), late 16th century. Opaque watercolor and shell gold on paper; image: 19.8 × 12.1 cm ($7\frac{13}{16}$ × $4\frac{3}{4}$ in.). The Art Institute of Chicago, Lucy Maud Buckingham Collection, 1919.951.

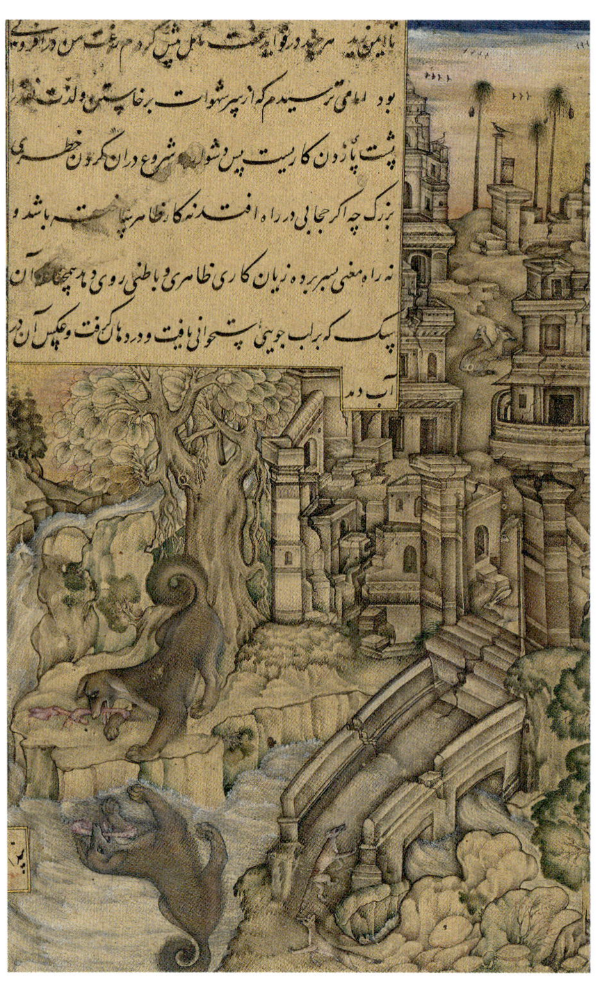

Greedy Dog (fig. 12).[54] Seeing his own reflection with a juicy bone in his mouth, the dog jumps into the stream to snatch his reflection's bone and drowns. The story is an allegory for people who give up what they have in desire of what they believe they lack; these desires are often not everything they appear to be.

Is *Paradise Lost* Shaw's own fable, retelling the tale of the Greedy Dog? Ripped from Kashmir's storied beauty and thrust into the temptations of the West, Shaw has realized that life is but a glittering mirage. By casting himself as Narcissus, he showed that he has learned his lesson and painted *Paradise Lost* to share his knowledge about desire, greed, name and fame, and all the world's many vices. In maturity, Shaw has observed the world from a distance, giving each character he has encountered a different animal's head according to their attributes. Disguised in the trees at the end of *Paradise Lost*, his self-portrait laughs as the cliff—and the illusion—begins to crumble.

Paradise Lost plays with illusion throughout, muddling it with reality to the point of confusion. But as the Indian scriptures say, life itself is *maya*, just an illusion, gone in a second. In the end, we can build our paradises wherever we want. The idealized paradise never existed in reality. Shaw lost his own paradise as the result of trauma both personal and political. Though his exile is self-imposed, his voice as a Kashmiri artist—typically absent from all discourse, erased, nameless, and scattered from the homeland—is vitally important to the current moment. His experience, and *Paradise Lost*, bears witness to the profound impact of loss—of one's homeland, family, and sense of self—but also how to heal from these absences. And yet he transmits his message in a Kashmiri manner: "In Kashmir metaphor is intrinsic to the way people speak and think . . . and it is through metaphor rather than directness that meaning is conveyed."[55] *Paradise Lost* ultimately calls viewers to turn within, to give up attachments, and to not fall for the glittering facade. Shaw forces each one of us encountering *Paradise Lost* to dig beneath its alluring surface as we search for our own paradise.

NOTES

1 Raqib Shaw, audio self-recording, Apr. 2025, Art Institute of Chicago.

2 Raqib Shaw quoted in Jon Lowe, *Raqib Shaw: Paradise Lost*, White Cube, 2011, https://vimeo.com/788259171/f86e8ea24a.

3 Raqib Shaw, "Artist's Perspective: Raqib Shaw discusses his exhibition at the Frist Art Museum," Frist Art Museum, YouTube, Sept. 18, 2023, 1 hr., 16 min, https://www.youtube.com/watch?v=wi7692Y6pVI.

4 For more on Shaw's Western art historical sources, see Dawn Ades, "On Pleasure and Pain," in *Raqib Shaw*, ed. Honey Luard (Rizzoli Electa, 2024), 61; and David Lomas in this volume.

5 Raqib Shaw, *Tales from an Urban Garden* (Raqib Shaw, 2022), 8–11; see also Jackie Wullschlager, "Inside Raqib Shaw's Fantasy Factory," *Financial Times*, Apr. 22, 2016, 11; and Shaw, "Artist's Perspective," Sept. 18, 2023.

6 *Firdaus* originated in Arabic and derives from the Old Persian *paridaiza*. It translates to *paradise* or *garden*. In the Islamic context, it refers to the highest level of paradise, *jannatul firdaus*, which is considered to be closest to God. *Jannat* also refers to paradise and is derived from the Arabic *jannah*, literally meaning garden or paradise. Today it tends to be used as a synonym for Kashmir's beauty.

7 While many have associated this couplet with the Mughal emperor Jahangir, it was actually composed by the Sufi poet Amir Khusrau Dehlavi (1253–1325) to describe India. See Ananya Jahanara Kabir, *Territory of Desire: Representing the Valley of Kashmir* (University of Minnesota Press, 2009), 212, n. 17; and Annemarie Schimmel, "The Celestial Garden in Islam," in *The Islamic Garden*, ed. Elisabeth B. Macdougall and Richard Ettinghausen (Dumbarton Oaks; Trustees for Harvard University, 1976), 20, n. 11.

8 The Mughals conquered Kashmir in 1586 when Emperor Akbar defeated the last independent king of Kashmir, Yakub Shah. Jahangir, his son and successor, described Kashmir's beauty in his memoirs, the *Jahangirnama*. Jahangir visited Kashmir regularly in his later years and died there on October 29, 1627. See Wheeler M. Thackston, *The Jahangirnama: Memoirs of Jahangir, Emperor of India* (Oxford University Press; The Freer Gallery of Art and the Arthur M. Sackler Gallery, 1999), xix, 70–71, 310–11, 331–35.

9 See Thackston, *Jahangirnama*, 331–35, for Jahangir's description of its flowers, fruits, geography, and people. Jahangir's favorite court artist, Mansur (see fig. 7), was commissioned to paint over one hundred flowers from the valley during the emperor's first spring visit in 1620.

10 See Barbara Schmitz, "Émigré Artists of Kashmir, 1585–1660," in *Orientations* 38, no. 7 (October 2007): 40–47; and Linda York Leach, "Painting in Kashmir from 1600 to 1650," in *Facets of Indian Art: A Symposium Held at the Victoria and Albert Museum on 26, 27, 28 April and 1 May 1982*, ed. Robert Skelton et al. (Victoria and Albert Museum, 1986), 124–31, on Kashmiri artists patronized by the Mughals.

11 For more on Islamic gardens, see Macdougall and Ettinghausen, *The Islamic Garden*. Jahangir constructed the Shalimar Bagh in Srinagar in 1616 for Empress Nur Jahan and called it Farah Bakhsh ("the delightful"). It was extended by his son Shah Jahan in 1632. The empress's brother Asaf Khan created the Nishat Bagh in 1632. Jahangir also created the octagonal pool at Nila Bagh in Verinag, and Princess Jahanara is said to have extended the gardens at Achabal nearby, originally built by Nur Jahan. The Chashme Shahi garden by the Dal Lake was laid out by a Mughal governor, Ali Mardan Khan, during the reign of Shah Jahan. For more on Mughal paradise gardens, see Elizabeth B. Moynihan, *Paradise as a Garden in Persia and Mughal India* (George Braziller, 1979); James L. Wescoat Jr. and Joachim Wolschke-Bulmahn, eds., *Mughal Gardens: Sources, Places, Representations, and Prospects* (Dumbarton Oaks Research Library and Collection, 1996), and for the Mughal gardens in Kashmir, see George Michell and Amit Pasricha, *Mughal Architecture and Gardens* (Shoestring, 2011), 308–43. See also Shaw, *Tales from an Urban Garden*, 8–10, where he discusses the impact of Mughal gardens in Kashmir on his work.

12 For more on the mystic poet Lal Ded, or Lalleshwari (c. 1320–1389) and the Sufi sheikh Nuruddin Nurani (1376–1438), popularly known as Nund Rishi, see Pratapaditya Pal, *The Arts of Kashmir* (Asia Society, 2007), 27; and Chitralekha Zutshi, *Languages of Belonging: Islam, Regional Identity and the Making of Kashmir* (Oxford University Press, 2004), 18–28. Also, Shaw, "Artist's Perspective," Sept. 18, 2023, describes the distinctive Sufism that prevailed in the valley.

13 For Kashmiriyat, see Kabir, *Territory of Desire*, 10; and Zutshi, *Languages of Belonging*, 2, 18–19, 211.

14 For a brief summary of the history of Kashmir, see Pal, *Arts of Kashmir*, 17–43, 115–25.

15 A timeline of the major events in the valley can be found in Chitralekha Zutshi, *Sheikh Abdullah: The Caged Lion of Kashmir* (Yale University Press, 2024), ix–xvii.

16 The Line of Control is the de facto border that has divided Indian- and Pakistan-administered Kashmir since 1948; China occupies the northeast section. Kabir, *Territory of Desire*, 7. For a map of the disputed areas, see Zutshi, *Languages of Belonging*, 313, map 3.

17 For a summary of the events of 1989–90, see Zutshi, *Sheikh Abdullah*, xvii.

18 Shaw's family moved from Kashmir to New Delhi in 1990 when Shaw was sixteen. He moved to Britain in 1993 at age eighteen. For Shaw's upbringing, education, and departure from the valley, see Patrick Elliott, *Raqib Shaw: Reinventing the Old Masters* (National Galleries of Scotland, 2018), 7–8; Arne Glimcher, "A Facetime Interview Between Arne Glimcher and Raqib Shaw," in *Raqib Shaw: Landscapes* (Pace Gallery, 2019), 7; and Zera Jumabhoy, "Raqib Shaw: The 'Happy Prince,'" in *Sangam/Confluence*, exh. cat. (Art House, Nita Mukesh Ambani Cultural Centre, Mumbai, India, 2023), 116.

19 "We carry our own minds everywhere, and that is the biggest prison." Raqib Shaw, "Artist Conversation: Raqib Shaw," Art Institute of Chicago, YouTube, June 7, 2025, 54 min., 27 sec., https://www.youtube.com/watch?v=9KUw2RsvYmQ.

20 See Raqib Shaw, "Raqib Shaw: Isolated Renaissance," National Galleries of Scotland, YouTube, 2018, 8 min., 30 sec., https://www.nationalgalleries.org/exhibition/raqib-shaw-reinventing-the-old-masters; and Dominic Gilday, dir., *Raqib Shaw: A Lost Home*, Bloomsday Films and White Cube, 2022.

21 For Shaw's unique painting technique, see Shaw, "Artist Conversation," June 7, 2025; Elliott, *Reinventing the Old Masters*, 8–9, 12, 22; Glimcher, "Facetime Interview," 2–3; and Ades, "On Pleasure and Pain," 61.

22 Shaw, "Artist's Perspective," Sept. 18, 2023.

23 For papier-mâché, see Kabir, *Territory of Desire*, 110–11, 119. Some contemporary Kashmiri artists, such as Veer Munshi and Fayaz Ahmad Jan, have recently started to use papier-mâché in their work. Artists from outside the valley, such as Praneet Soi, have also employed it in their artwork.

24 The valley was long associated with the production of many kinds of handicrafts, the most famous of which is the ubiquitous cashmere shawl, whose popularity reached its zenith in nineteenth-century France, leading to mechanized imitations. For a short summary, see Frank Ames, "Woven Legends: Carpets and Shawls of Kashmir (1585–1870)," in Pal, *Arts of Kashmir*, 193–209. See Kabir, *Territory of Desire*, 119; and Pal, *Arts of Kashmir*, 18, fig. 1, and 175–209, on Kashmiri crafts.

25 For a summary of painting in Kashmir, see Pal, *Arts of Kashmir*, 100–113, 146–73.

26 Raqib Shaw, conversation with the author, Jan. 26, 2025.

27 See Shaw, "Artist Conversation," June 7, 2025, for a discussion of Kashmiri decorative traditions and how they have influenced his aesthetics.

28 Shaw, conversation with the author, Jan. 26, 2025.

29 The term "humanoid" for this animal-headed creature was first used by Homi K. Bhabha, "An Art of Exquisite Anxiety," in *Raqib Shaw: Absence of God* (White Cube; Kunsthalle Wien, 2009), 5–11, particularly 6.

30 Shaw first painted this figure in the *Absence of God* series (2007–9). See *Absence of God II* (2008), 36–37, and *Absence of God VI* (2009), 52–53, in Luard, *Raqib Shaw* (2024).

31 Shaw, "Artist Conversation," June 7, 2025.

32 Shaw, recording, Apr. 2025; and Shaw, conversation with the author, Jan. 26, 2025.

33 Shaw, recording, Apr. 2025.

34 For one such Kashmiri example, see Pal, *Arts of Kashmir*, 159, fig. 171, of Isfandiyar fighting a simurgh from a copy of Firdausi's *Shahnama* published in 1731. Its current whereabouts are unknown.

35 The zebra was given to Jahangir in March 1621 at Nowruz, and he ordered Mansur, a court painter, to depict it. Jahangir wrote in his memoirs that he thought the animal's stripes were painted on. The emperor's inscription on the right side specifies that the artist was Mansur, and that the animal was brought from Ethiopia by Turks who accompanied the Mughal courtier Mir Ja'far. Since it was so rare, the zebra was included in the gifts Jahangir sent to the Safavid emperor Shah Abbas. See Thackston, *Jahangirnama*, 359–60; and Peter Jarman, "Plumes, Pets and *Pishkesh*: Exotic Animals and the Great Mughals," in *The Great Mughals: Art, Architecture and Opulence*, ed. Susan Stronge (Victoria and Albert Museum, 2024), 246–59, particularly 250–51, fig. 212.

36 Shaw recalls being "treated like a noble savage from Kashmir" when he arrived at college. Glimcher, "Facetime Interview," 2. Shaw has shared that he has felt like he never fit in anywhere from childhood. Shaw recounted that Kashmiris believe that the soul of a place gets into a person. According to his mother, he was born "by accident" in Calcutta; therefore, in Kashmir he was treated as an outsider. His relatively dark skin, in comparison to other Kashmiris, also made him stand out. Shaw, "Artist's Perspective," Sept. 18, 2023.

37 Composite animals and angels were particularly popular among the local artists in the eighteenth century. See Pal, *Arts of Kashmir*, 161, figs. 172–74.

38 *Nim kalam* or *siyah kalam* (meaning black pen) describes a style of monochromatic painting usually in black or dark brown ink with a limited use of color and a lot of shading; gold was used sparingly for highlights. Such painting became very popular in the Mughal and Deccani courts. A peri, derived from *pari*, may be equated with a fairy.

39 For more on this subject, see Robert J. Del Bonta, "Indian Composite Paintings: A Playful Art," *Orientations* 27, no. 1 (Jan. 1996): 31–38.

40 Shaw, recording, Apr. 2025. He calls these faces his "ugly mes." Shaw has discussed the masks we figuratively wear. Shaw, "Artist Conversation," June 7, 2025.

41 From the time of Shaw's *Self Portrait* series (2013–18), he started to paint himself as himself instead of as one of his avatars. See Honey Luard, ed., *Raqib Shaw: Self Portraits* (White Cube, 2016); and Luard, *Raqib Shaw* (2024), 107–43.

42 In the painting, Shaw's self-portrait writes: "But a humble scribe documenting the eternal deception of the firmament . . . A futile eponym of an author, as empty of alphabet, as sparse of knowledge . . . a mere medium of a collapsing conduit . . . corroding faster every second the wind whips up the fateful waves."

43 The portable shrine is by Shaw's side in *Self Portrait in the Study at Peckham (After Vincenzo Catena) Kashmir Version* (2015–16; private collection), published in Luard, *Raqib Shaw* (2024), 118–19. It is strange to associate Shaw, who grew up as a Muslim, with this home shrine, an exquisite example of Kashmiri metalwork, used to house images of Hindu deities: It is indicative of his expansive upbringing and education which made him into the epitome of the concept of the Kashmiriyat so cherished in the valley. See also Pal, *Arts of Kashmir*, 184, 188, fig. 207. Shaw painted the silver attardan in *The Adoration (After Jan Gossaert)* (fig. 3, p. 29). There was a devastating fire in Shaw's studio in 2017. He later ceremoniously burned his beloved heirloom shawl, depicted in *The Final Submission in Fire on Ice* (fig. 10, p. 35).

44 Shaw's triptych *Garden of Earthly Delights III* (2003) sold at Sotheby's in London for nearly $5.5 million on Oct. 12, 2007. This sale brought him unwanted attention. Shaw, "Artist's Perspective," Sept. 18, 2023.

45 Shaw notes: "Home is a memory of a place and a time that existed back then, and it doesn't really exist anymore." Gilday, *A Lost Home*, 2022; and Shaw, "Artist's Perspective," Sept. 18, 2023.

46 Shaw painted the same marble palace in *Ode to the Valley of Wonderment* (2017–18; Metropolitan Museum of Art, New York) and in *Allegory of the Spirit* (2016–18; private collection), both published in Luard, *Raqib Shaw* (2024), 159–61. The Mughal Panch Mahal at Fatehpur Sikri could be the inspiration, see Michell and Pasricha, *Mughal Architecture*, 222–23.

47 Shaw felt he had not experienced real sorrow until he faced the loss of his beloved Mr C in 2021 as well as the death of his cousin. Gilday, *A Lost Home*, 2022; and Shaw, "Artist's Perspective," Sept. 18, 2023.

48 Shaw quoted in Gilday, *A Lost Home*, 2022. The passage reads: "The man who forsakes all objects of desire and goes about without cravings, possessiveness, and self-centeredness becomes serene." *The Bhagavadgita in the Mahabharata*, ed. and trans. by J. A. B. van Buitenen (University of Chicago Press, 1981), 80–81, line 24[2]70.

49 For more on the mystic poet Lal Ded, see Zutshi, *Languages of Belonging*, 18–28.

50 The verse quoted here is attributed to Lal Ded and remembered, interpreted, and translated by Raqib Shaw in Luard, *Raqib Shaw* (2024), 15. This source incorrectly identifies Lal Ded as a seventeenth-century mystic.

51 Chaupar (or *chausar*) is played on a cross-shaped cloth with elongated dice. For more, see W. Norman Brown, "The Indian Games of Pachisi, Chaupar, and Chausar," *Expedition Magazine* 6, no. 3 (May 1964): 32–35; and Andrew Topsfield, "Dice, Chaupar, Chess: Indian Games in History, Myth, Poetry, and Art," in Andrew Topsfield, ed., *The Art of Play: Board and Card Games of India* (Marg, 2006), 11–31.

52 Japanese influences can be seen across Shaw's practice; he loved Japanese prints while growing up, and some of his early works were inspired by Katsushika Hokusai. Shaw, "Artist Conversation," June 7, 2025. He was inspired by the Japanese way of thinking and the idea of *monozukuri*, or dedicating one's life to the pursuit of beauty through craft and discipline. Shaw, recording, Apr. 2025. His affinity for Japan is also reflected in his vast kimono collection and expertise in bonsai and ikebana.

53 This section of *Paradise Lost* is based almost entirely on Shaw's painting *From Narcissus to Icarus . . . A Summer Odyssey* (fig. 12, p. 39), but here Shaw changed the flowing brook to a cliff. For more on the relationship to this work, see David Lomas's essay in this volume.

54 The story originated in a lost manuscript of animal fables known as the *Panchatantra* in India and was eventually adapted into European bestiary, including *Aesop's Fables*. This particular page may be from the *Anvar-i Suhayli*, translated into Persian and illustrated in the imperial atelier of the Mughal emperor Akbar (reigned 1556–1605). It has been attributed to the artist Farrukh Chela (active 1580–1604). The story originated sometime in the second to sixth centuries.

55 Shaw, recording, Apr. 2025.

About the Installation

MADHUVANTI GHOSE

In the Art Institute of Chicago's Alsdorf Galleries, sculptures from across South Asia enriched the experience of viewing Raqib Shaw's monumental painting *Paradise Lost*.[1] They spoke to the vibrant Hindu and Buddhist past of Shaw's homeland, the Kashmir Valley. Visitors entering the galleries from the east were met by the six-headed, twelve-armed sculpture of Karttikeya, the commander of the divine armies, seated on his peacock, ready to go to war. His many arms and heads denote his superhuman power. Karttikeya's placement near the beginning of Shaw's painting referred to the war and strife that has beset the Kashmir Valley.

The goddess Saraswati also greeted visitors near the east end of the painting. Here, she represents Sharada, the goddess of the arts, knowledge, learning, and wisdom, revered in the Kashmir Valley since ancient times, especially by Hindu pandits. Kashmir was home to a branch of Shaivism, represented by the four-faced Shiva *linga* (fig. 2) in front of the section of *Paradise Lost* that considers Shaw's early life. The linga, a phallic form, is Shiva's most sacred aspect and the main focus of worship in his temples. It symbolizes his control of the cosmic creative force. Nearby, the goddess Durga slays the buffalo demon Mahishasura (fig. 2). This sculpture indicated Shaw's birthplace, Calcutta, and the impact that its annual Durga Puja festival had on his artistic development.

At the west end of the painting, visitors saw various images of the god Vishnu, the preserver of the universe and, like Shiva, one of Hinduism's principal deities. When cosmic order is imperiled, Vishnu descends to earth in different avatars to restore it. Varaha, Vishnu's boar incarnation (fig. 1), sits near the last section of *Paradise Lost*. According to Hindu mythology, when the demon Hiranyaksha hid the earth in the primeval ocean, Varaha rescued it, emerging triumphantly with the earth goddess Bhudevi on his tusk. Bhudevi, standing at the boar's head, symbolizes plenitude and prosperity, which were restored by Varaha's rescue. The gods, sages, and animals carved in rows on his back venerate Vishnu for restoring order. In this avatar, Vishnu embodies the infinite nature of the cosmos.

A monolithic granite Buddha Shakyamuni (see p. 10) mirrored the Karttikeya at the west end of *Paradise Lost*. He hinted at Kashmir's rich Buddhist legacy: Buddhism flourished—alongside Hinduism—from at least the third century BCE and spread from Kashmir to Tibet, Central Asia, and eventually China. The Buddha sits in meditation, emblematic of the peace that remains out of reach in Kashmir.

1 For more information about these artworks, search for the following accession numbers on artic.edu: 1962.203, 2019.733, 2021.236, 2006.187, 2021.200, 2021.242, 2014.1026, and 1964.556.

OPPOSITE

1 Boar Incarnation of God Vishnu (Varaha), c. 10th century. Madhya Pradesh, India. Phyllite; 56 × 79.5 × 29.7 cm (22 1/16 × 31 5/16 × 11 11/16 in.). The Art Institute of Chicago, James W. and Marilynn Alsdorf Collection, gift of Marilynn Alsdorf, 2021.200.

FOLLOWING SPREAD

2 Installation view of *Paradise Lost*. In the foreground, from left: Emblem of God Shiva with Four Faces (*Chaturmukhalinga*), 7th–8th century. Rajasthan, India. Sandstone; 71.7 × 40.6 × 44 cm (28¼ × 16 × 17 5/16 in.). The Art Institute of Chicago, James W. and Marilynn Alsdorf Collection, gift of Marilynn Alsdorf, 2021.236; and Goddess Durga Slaying the Buffalo Demon (Mahishasuramardini), 6th century. India. Sandstone; 76.5 × 44.5 × 15 cm (30⅛ × 17½ × 5⅞ in.). The Art Institute of Chicago, gift of Marilynn B. Alsdorf, 2006.187.

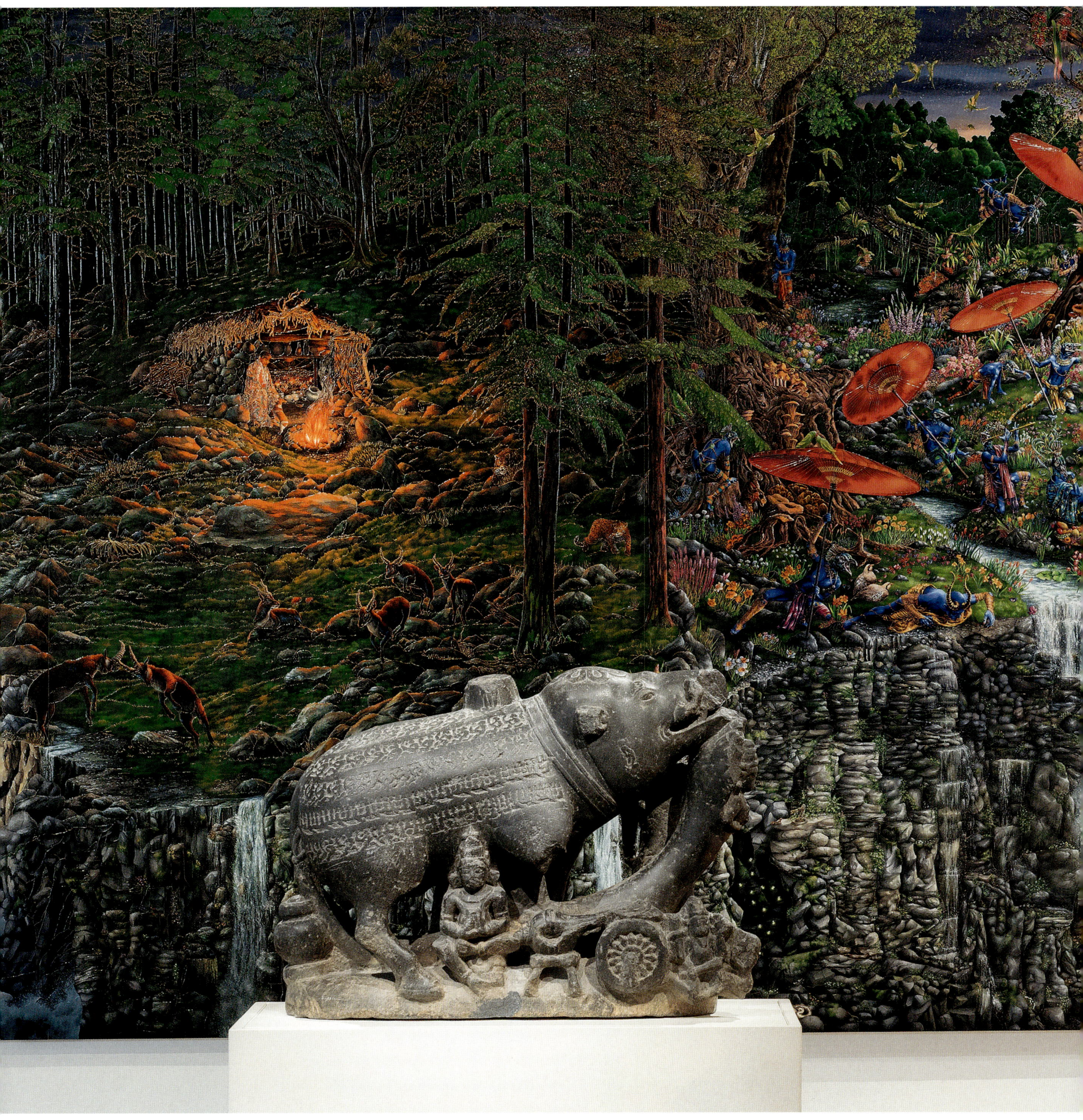

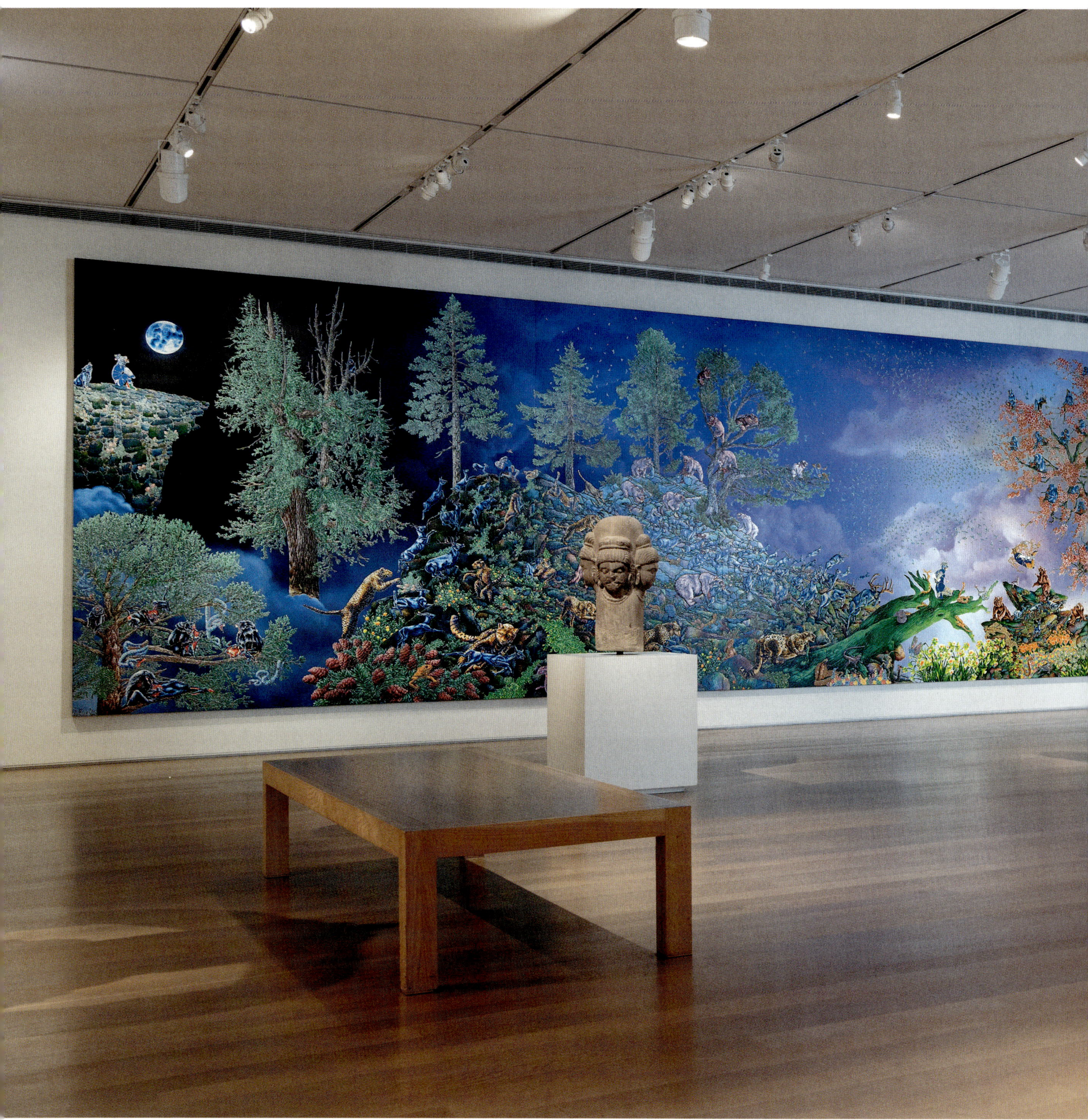

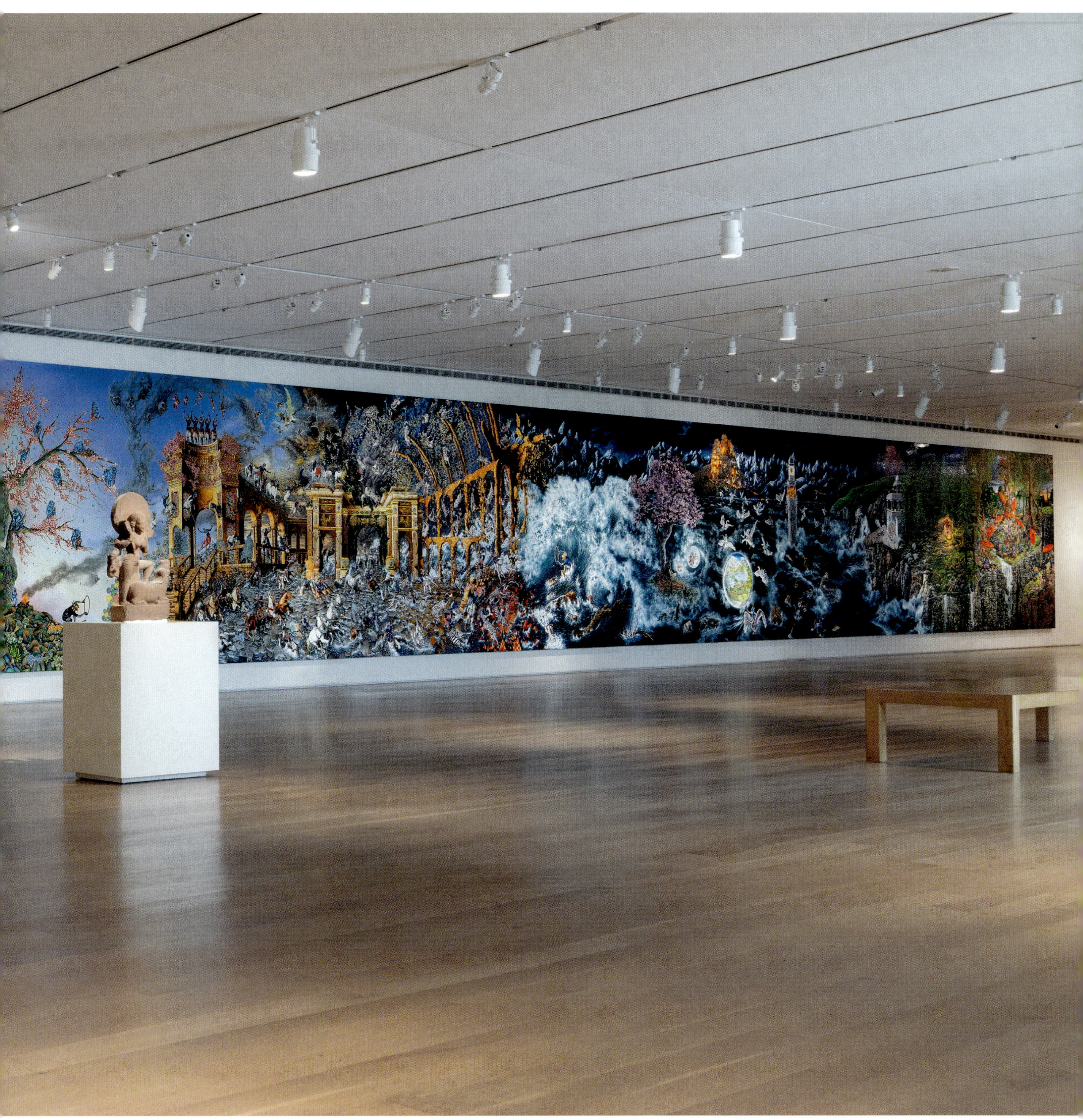

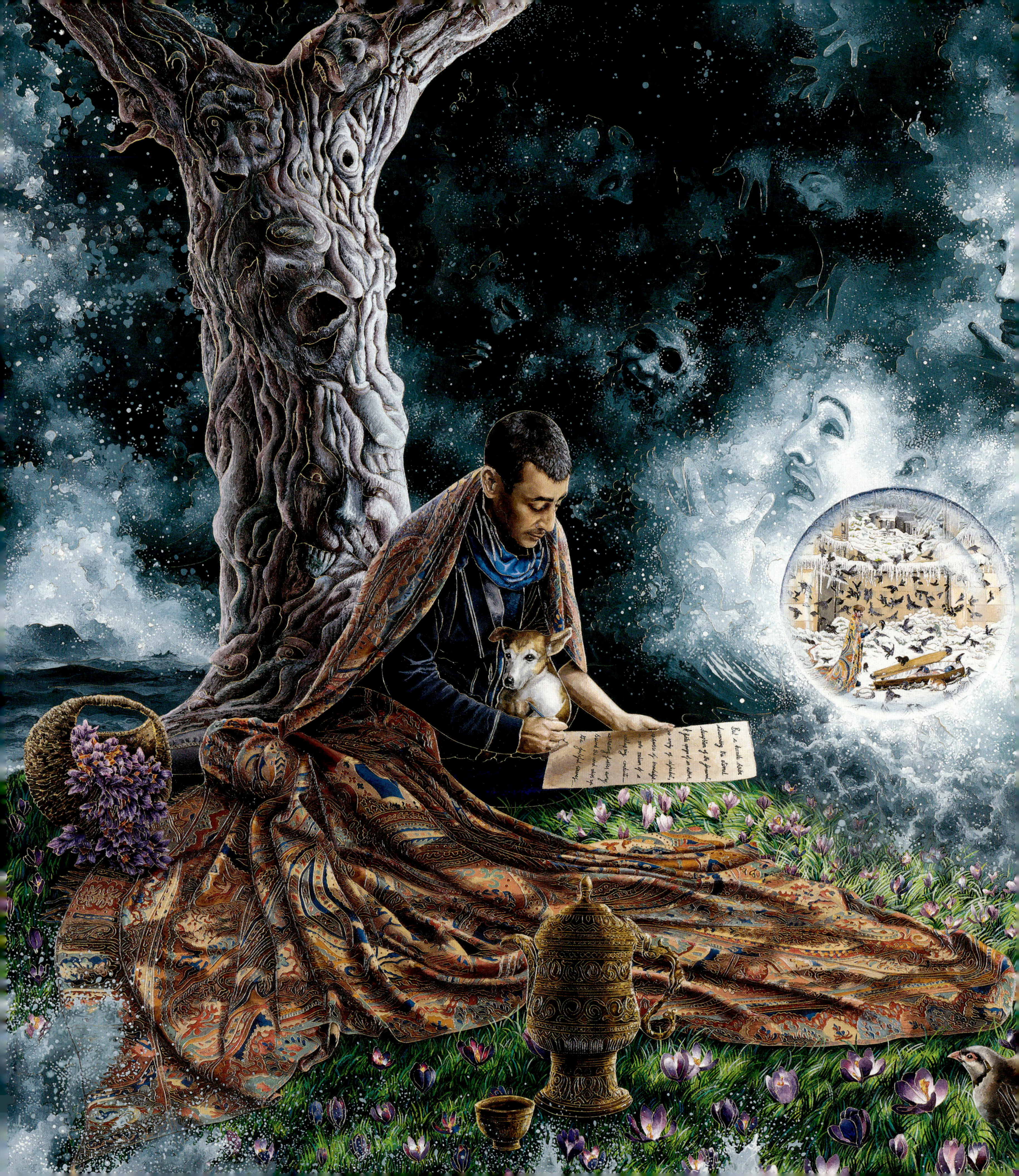
But a humble scribe
documenting the eternal

Books That Have Shaped Me

RAQIB SHAW

De Profundis by Oscar Wilde

Methuen & Co., 1913. First published in 1905; first published in full in 1949 by Methuen & Co.

Part prison letter, part spiritual reckoning, *De Profundis* is the most beautiful and devastating love letter I have ever read. In it, Wilde turns the brutality of his imprisonment into something luminous—an act of self-analysis so raw and refined that it becomes, paradoxically, a work of art. That tension—between beauty and pain—resonates with my own practice. Wilde's meditations on suffering, on love warped by vanity, and, most poignantly, on the act of forgiveness ("I must forgive him for my own sake") possess a clarity that borders on the sacred. And then there is the passage on Christ—Wilde's Christ—not as dogma but as the purest embodiment of human vulnerability and imagination. I return to that passage often. It reads not like religion, but revelation.

The Complete Novels and Plays of "Saki"

[H. H. Munro]. The Bodley Head, 1949. Originally published in 1933 by Viking Press.

I first met Saki in a schoolroom in Kashmir, through "Mrs. Packletide's Tiger"—and I've never quite recovered. His stories are like perfectly cut gemstones: dazzling, razor-edged, and wickedly funny. Beneath the comedy lies a masterful study of human nature—the vanity, the pettiness, the quiet cruelties—all cloaked in the elegance of Edwardian wit. His portrayals of colonial India are absurd and astute in equal measure, revealing the hypocrisies of empire with a lightness of touch that still leaves me laughing aloud. No one skewers social pretension quite like Saki, and few writers understand the theater of human behavior so instinctively. For all their mischief, his stories are, at their heart, exquisite little portraits of the human condition—and I return to them, always, for delight.

Things Seen in Kashmir by Ernest Frederic Neve

Seeley, Service & Co., 1931.

This book is more than a historical document—it is a breath of air from a Kashmir that now only exists in memory and imagination. Ernest Frederic Neve wrote with a rare tenderness, capturing the daily rhythms, beliefs, and quiet dignity of a people untouched by modernity. His tone is never distant; it is intimate, observant, and alive with affection. As I read, I can smell the air of home, feel the softness of the light on the mountains, and glimpse a time when innocence was not yet a myth. Neve was more than an observer—he was a healer, an educator, a servant of the people. His discovery of the link between the kangri [a Kashmiri portable heater] and cancer saved countless lives, and his introduction of Western medicine and education laid a foundation for generations to come. For anyone who longs to understand Kashmir—not as an idea, but as a living soul—this book is essential.

Man and His Symbols by Carl Jung

Edited by M.-L. von Franz. Pan Books, 1978. Originally published in 1964 by Doubleday.

I first encountered Carl Jung in my teens, then again in my thirties, and now—as I return to his writings yet again—the same sentences reveal entirely different meanings. It is as though the book ages with me, or rather, I age into the book. *Man and His Symbols* feels less like a reading experience and more like a remembering. Jung's assertion that the universe and the individual are not separate but deeply entangled echoes something I've always known intuitively, growing up in Kashmir—where ancient wisdom is not taught but lived, sung, and woven into the myths that lace the landscape. Long before I had ever heard Jung's name, I had already met his ideas in the stories of saints and seers told to me as a child. His explorations of the anima and animus, his reverence for the dreamworld, and his dialogue with the East make him, in my view, not merely a psychologist but one of the great philosophers of our age—a bridge between inner worlds and outer forms, not unlike art itself.

The Works of Shakespeare

Imperial Edition, edited by Charles Knight, 2 vols. London, c. 1873.

Bound in worn leather and weighted with history, my copy of Imperial Shakespeare is more than a book—it is, to me, the Bible of literature. William Shakespeare remains the most celebrated bard the world has ever known, and rightly so: No one has captured the human soul in language so enduring, so precise, and so devastatingly beautiful. Among all his works, it is *Macbeth* that lingers with me most. That great soliloquy—"Tomorrow and tomorrow and tomorrow . . ."—is perhaps the purest distillation of time, mortality, and the quiet futility of human ambition. It reads like a dirge for all of us, and yet there is something transcendent in its sorrow. This edition, edited by Charles Knight, feels sacred in my hands—a portal to the stage, to the shadowy corridors of the mind, and to the timeless theater of our lives.

Orientalism by Edward Said

Modern Classics, Penguin Books, 2007. Originally published in 1978 by Pantheon Books.

My very first college seminar was on *Orientalism*, and it was like being handed a lens I had always needed but had never known existed. Edward Said's voice—incisive, eloquent, and unsparingly honest—feels even more urgent today than when I first encountered it. His deconstruction of the "Oriental" as a projection of Western fantasy struck me deeply, not least because I had already begun to feel its quiet violence. For much of my time at university, I was treated—however politely—as a kind of noble savage: exotic, decorative, slightly other. Said gave language to that experience. And coming from Kashmir, a region so often spoken for, romanticized, or reduced, his reflections on selfhood, representation, and cultural power resonated like a private truth made public. *Orientalism* is not simply a critique of the past—it is a call to remain vigilant, to keep asking who is speaking, and for whom.

Editor's note: The citations here reflect the editions in Raqib Shaw's library.

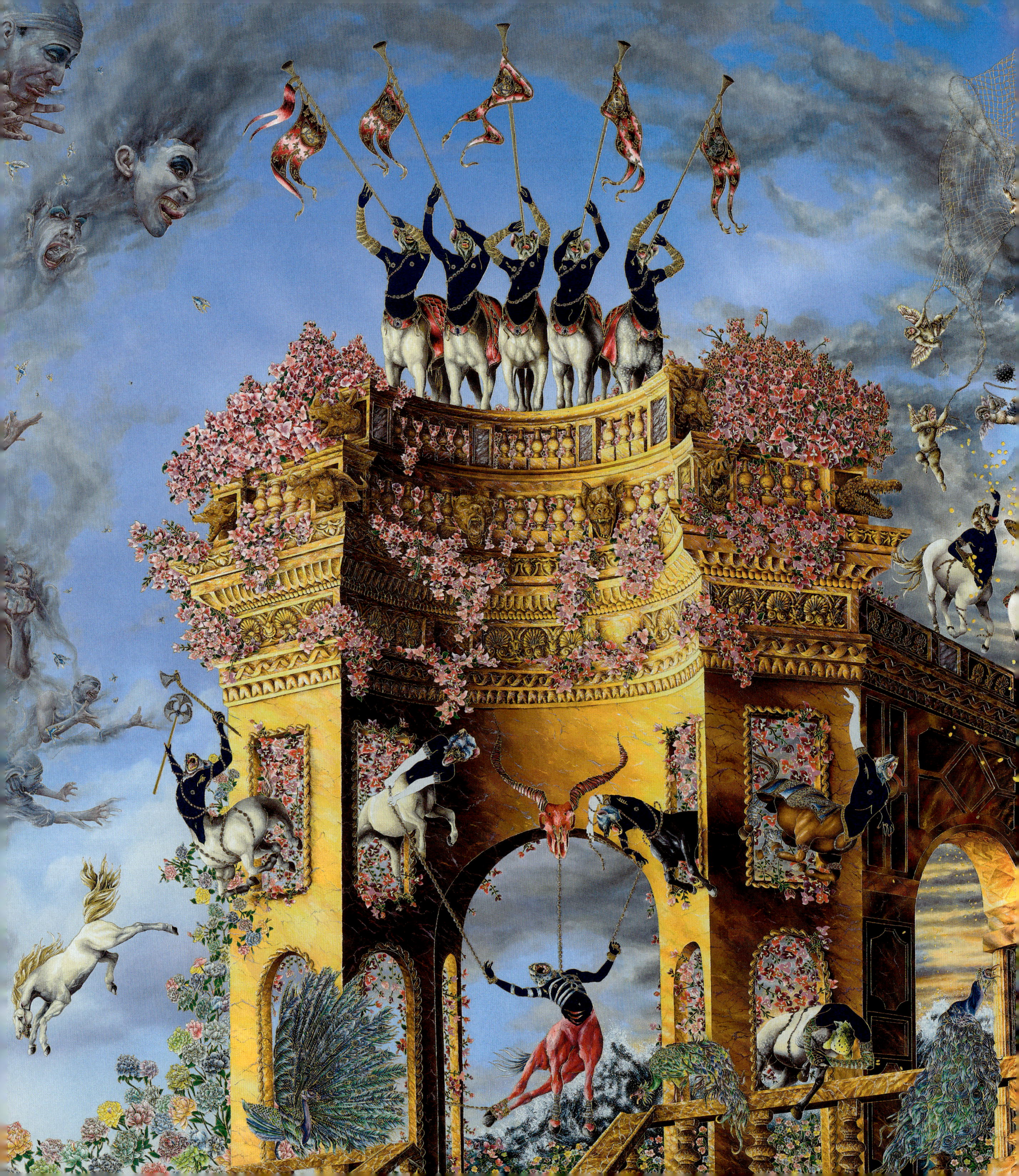

Contributors

MADHUVANTI GHOSE is the inaugural Alsdorf Associate Curator of Indian, Southeast Asian, and Himalayan Art at the Art Institute of Chicago. Since joining the museum in 2007, she opened the Alsdorf Galleries in 2008 and has curated numerous exhibitions and installations, including Jitish Kallat's site-specific *Public Notice 3* (2010–11; 2024–26), *Gates of the Lord: The Tradition of Krishna Paintings* (2015–16), *Vanishing Beauty: Asian Jewelry and Ritual Objects from the Barbara and David Kipper Collection* (2016), and *India Modern: The Paintings of M. F. Husain* (2017–18).

DAVID LOMAS is emeritus professor of art history at the University of Manchester. He has published extensively on surrealism, psychology, and medicine, including the book *The Haunted Self: Surrealism, Psychoanalysis, Subjectivity* (Yale University Press, 2000). A longtime admirer of the work of Raqib Shaw, he wrote for the catalogue of the 2011 White Cube exhibition *Paradise Lost*.

JAMES RONDEAU is the President and Eloise W. Martin Director of the Art Institute of Chicago. His recent curatorial projects include *Tomma Abts* (2018–19) and *Barbara Kruger: THINKING OF ~~YOU~~. I MEAN ~~ME~~. I MEAN YOU.* (2021).

RAQIB SHAW constructs intricately layered compositions that move between meditative calm and dynamic intensity using an innovative and distinctive technique: drawing enamel with porcupine quills. Shaw's paintings engage with both personal experience and broader cultural discourse, drawing on a wide spectrum of influences that include Renaissance painting; Japanese aesthetics; Persian, Mughal, and Hindu art forms; Western literature; and Jungian philosophy. Employing metaphor and satire, Shaw addresses the complexities of contemporary existence and the enduring questions of the human condition. Shaw has had solo exhibitions at Museum of Contemporary Art, North Miami, FL (2006); Tate Britain, London (2006); Metropolitan Museum of Art, New York (2008); Kunsthalle Wien, Vienna (2009); Manchester Art Gallery, England (2013); Galerie Rudolfinum, Prague (2013), National Galleries of Scotland, Modern, Edinburgh (2018); Ca' Pesaro International Gallery of Modern Art, Venice, Italy (2022); Frist Art Museum, Nashville, TN (2023); Isabella Stewart Gardner Museum, Boston (2023); Museum of Fine Arts, Houston (2024); and the Huntington Art Museum, San Marino, CA (2024). Shaw was born in Calcutta, India, in 1974 and lives and works in London.

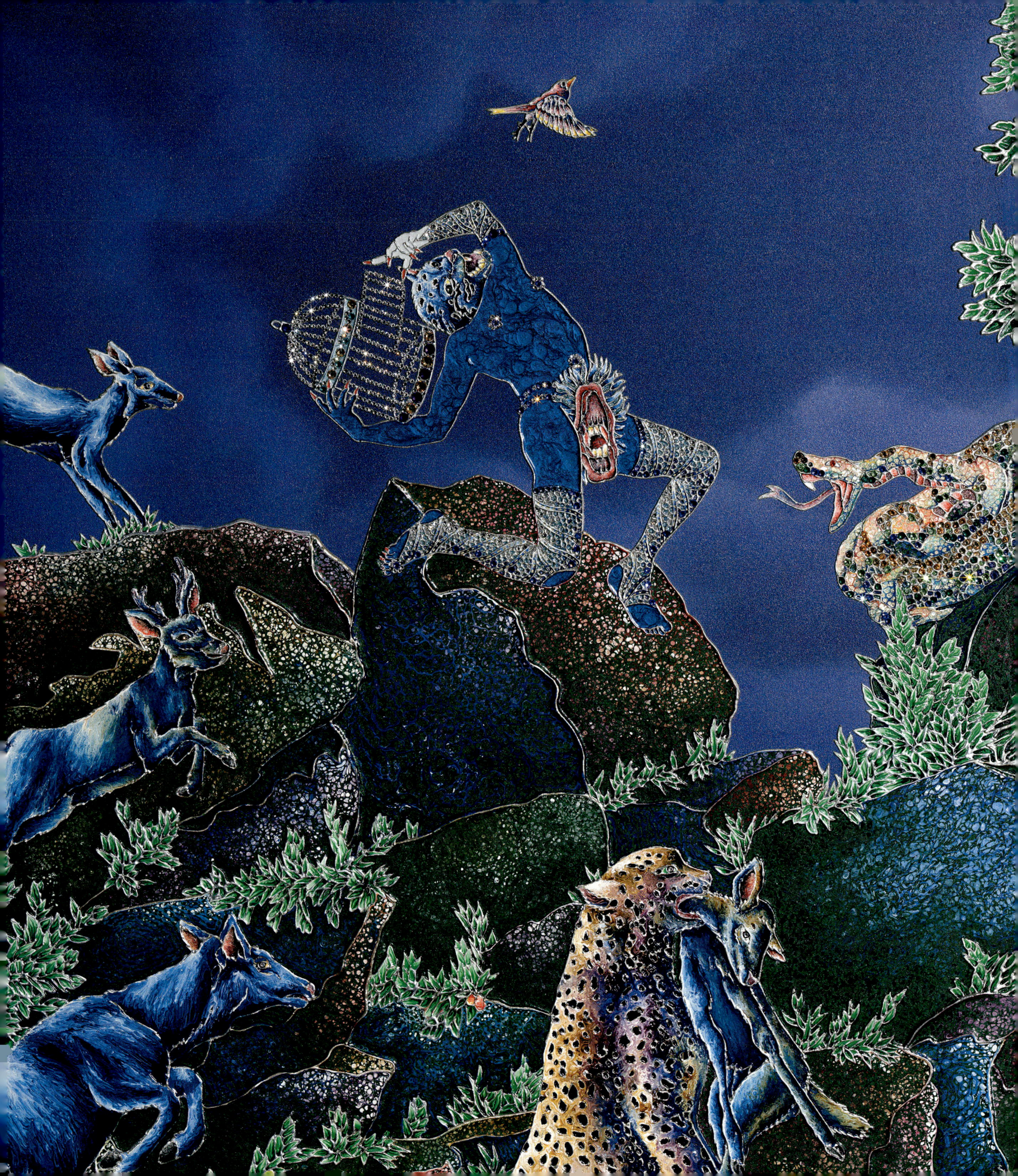

Index

Note: unless otherwise noted, all works are by Raqib Shaw; works by artists other than Shaw are found under the artist's name; page numbers in *italics* refer to illustrations.

Photography Credits

Unless otherwise noted, installation views and photographs of artworks in the collection are copyrighted by the Art Institute of Chicago. Photography by Nathan Keay, Robert Lifson, Jonathan Mathias, Juan Molina Hernández, and Joe Tallarico. Postproduction by Hayley Hinsberger and Kaitlyn Fultz-Campion.

Unless otherwise noted, photography of *Paradise Lost* is by Prudence Cuming, London.

All works by Raqib Shaw are © Raqib Shaw.

Every effort has been made to identify, contact, and acknowledge copyright holders for all reproductions; additional rights holders are encouraged to contact the Art Institute of Chicago. The following credits apply to all images in this book for which separate acknowledgment is due.

p. 4: Imaging, Art Institute of Chicago; p. 28, fig. 1: © Trustees of the British Museum; p. 29, fig. 3: Photo © White Cube (George Darrell); p. 30, fig. 4: Courtesy National Museums Liverpool, Walker Art Gallery; p. 31, fig. 5: Photo: bpk Bildagentur / National Museums in Berlin, National Gallery / Jörg P. Anders / Art Resource, NY; p. 32, fig. 6: Photo © President and Fellows of Harvard College; p. 35, fig. 9: Photo © White Cube (Theo Christelis); p. 39, fig. 12: Photo courtesy of Pace Gallery; p. 40, fig. 13: Image courtesy of Rijksmuseum, Amsterdam; p. 58, fig. 1: Photo © Amit Pasricha; p. 60, fig. 3: Photo by Dave Stamboulis / Alamy; p. 61: Imaging, Art Institute of Chicago; p. 63, fig. 7: V&A Images, London / Art Resource, NY; p. 65, figs. 9–10: Images courtesy of Raqib Shaw studio.

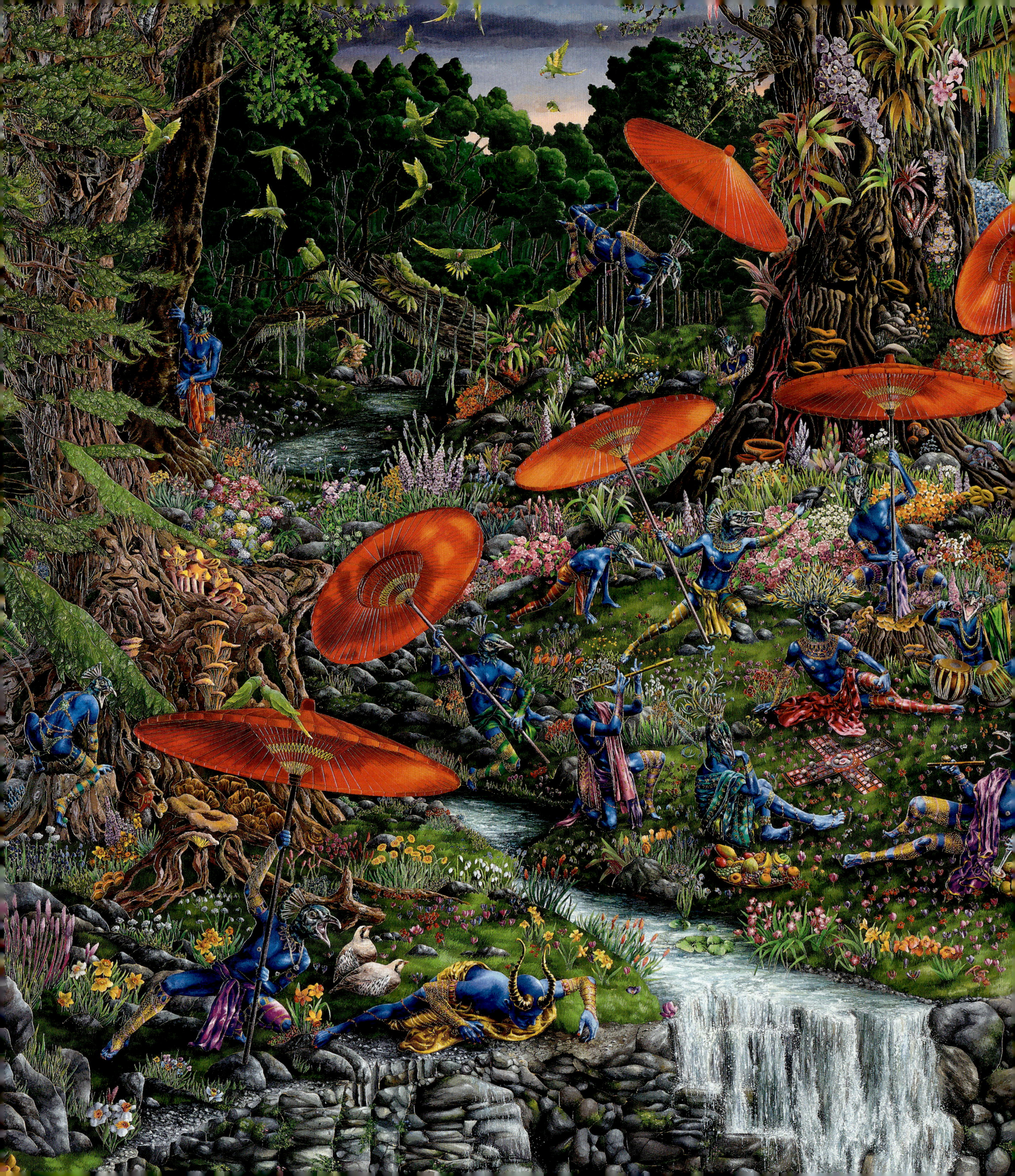

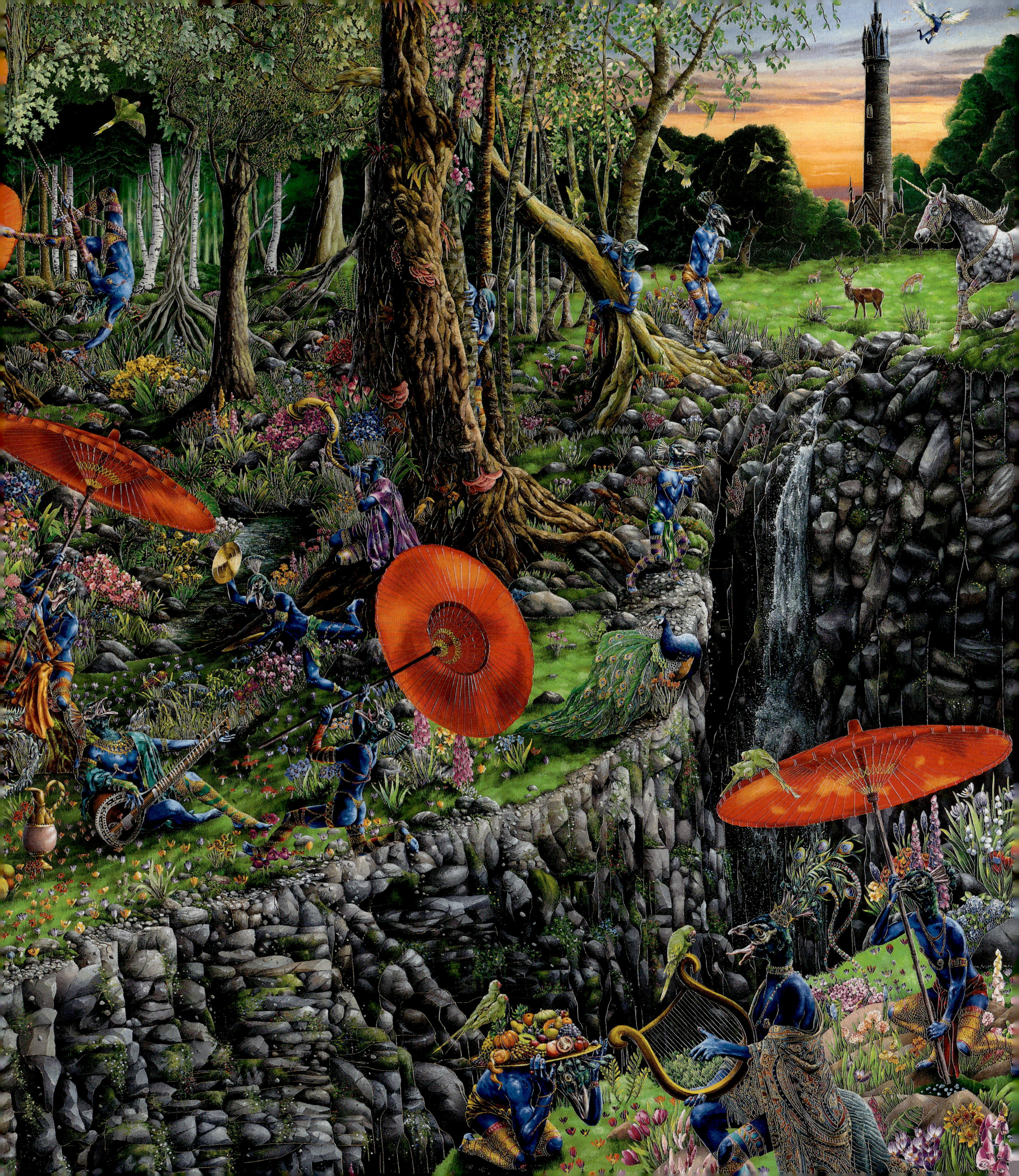

Raqib Shaw: Paradise Lost was published in conjunction with an exhibition of the same title organized by the Art Institute of Chicago, which opened on June 7, 2025.

Generous support for *Raqib Shaw: Paradise Lost* is provided by Usha and Lakshmi Niwas Mittal.

First edition
Printed in Spain
31 30 29 28 27 26   1 2 3 4 5

Authorized representative in the EU: Easy Access System Europe, Mustamäe tee 50, 10621 Tallinn, Estonia, gpsr.requests@easproject.com

ISBN: 978-0-300-28650-2 (hardcover)

Library of Congress Control Number: 2025948371

Published by
The Art Institute of Chicago
111 South Michigan Avenue
Chicago, IL 60603-6404
artic.edu

Distributed by
Yale University Press
302 Temple Street
P. O. Box 209040
New Haven, CT 06520-9040
yalebooks.com/art

Edited by Kati Woock
Production by Elizabeth Upenieks with Lauren Makholm
Photography research by Kristie Kahns
Proofreading by David B. Olsen
Indexing by Barbara Smith
Design by Julia Ma, Miko McGinty Inc.
Typesetting in Halyard Display and Söhne by Tina Henderson, Miko McGinty Inc.
Separations by Professional Graphics, Rockford, Illinois
Printing and binding by SYL, Barcelona

Publishing, the Art Institute of Chicago
Katie Reilly, Associate Vice President, Publishing
Lisa Meyerowitz, Editorial Director
Lauren Makholm, Director of Production

Imaging, the Art Institute of Chicago
Bonnie Rosenberg, Director of Imaging
Nathan Keay, Associate Director, Photography
Elyse M. Allen, Associate Director, Production

Cover and details: Raqib Shaw, *Paradise Lost*, 2009–25

This book was made using paper and materials certified by the Forest Stewardship Council, which ensures responsible forest management.

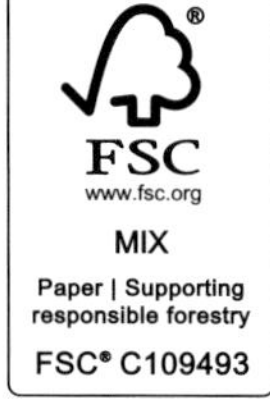

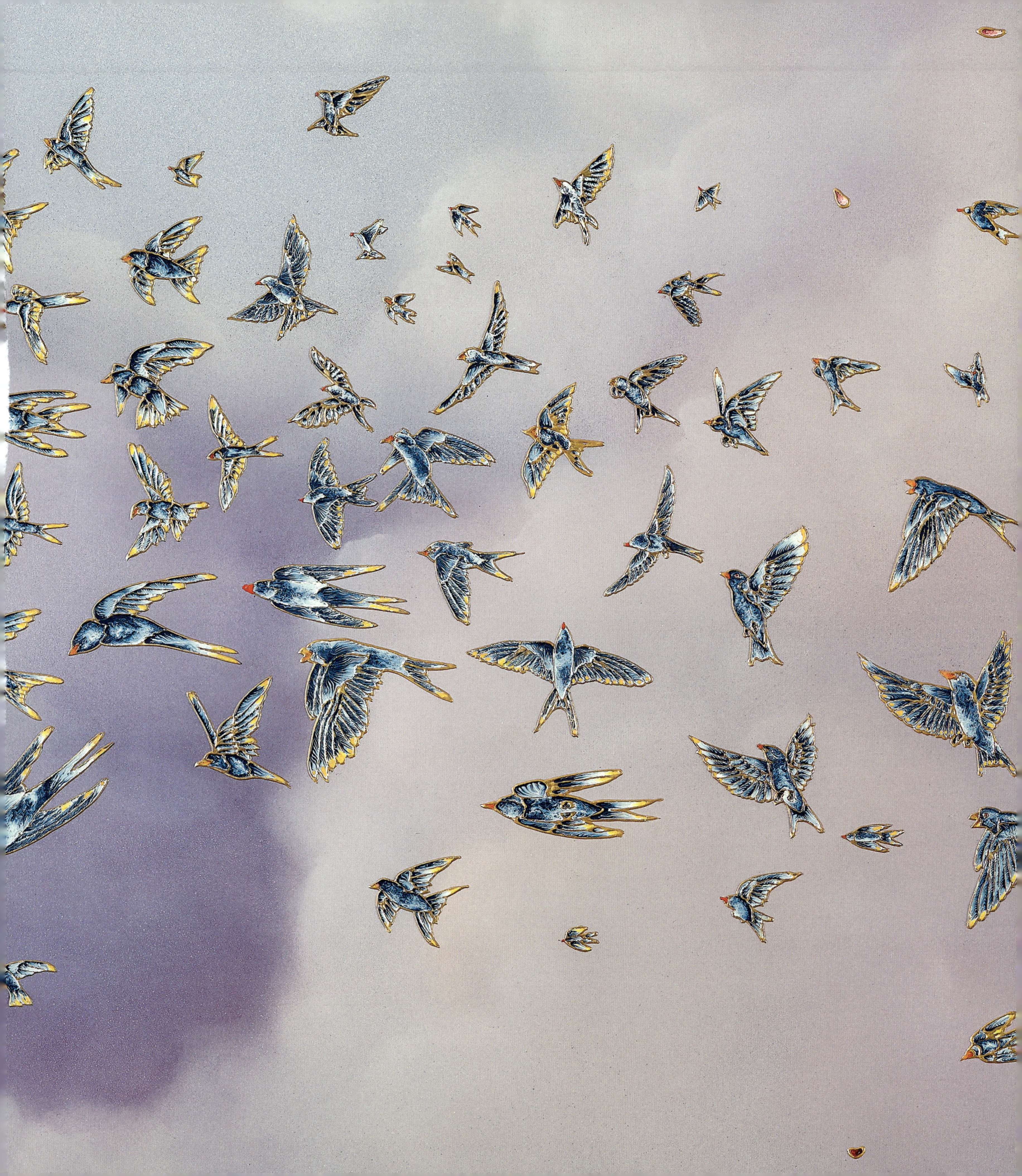

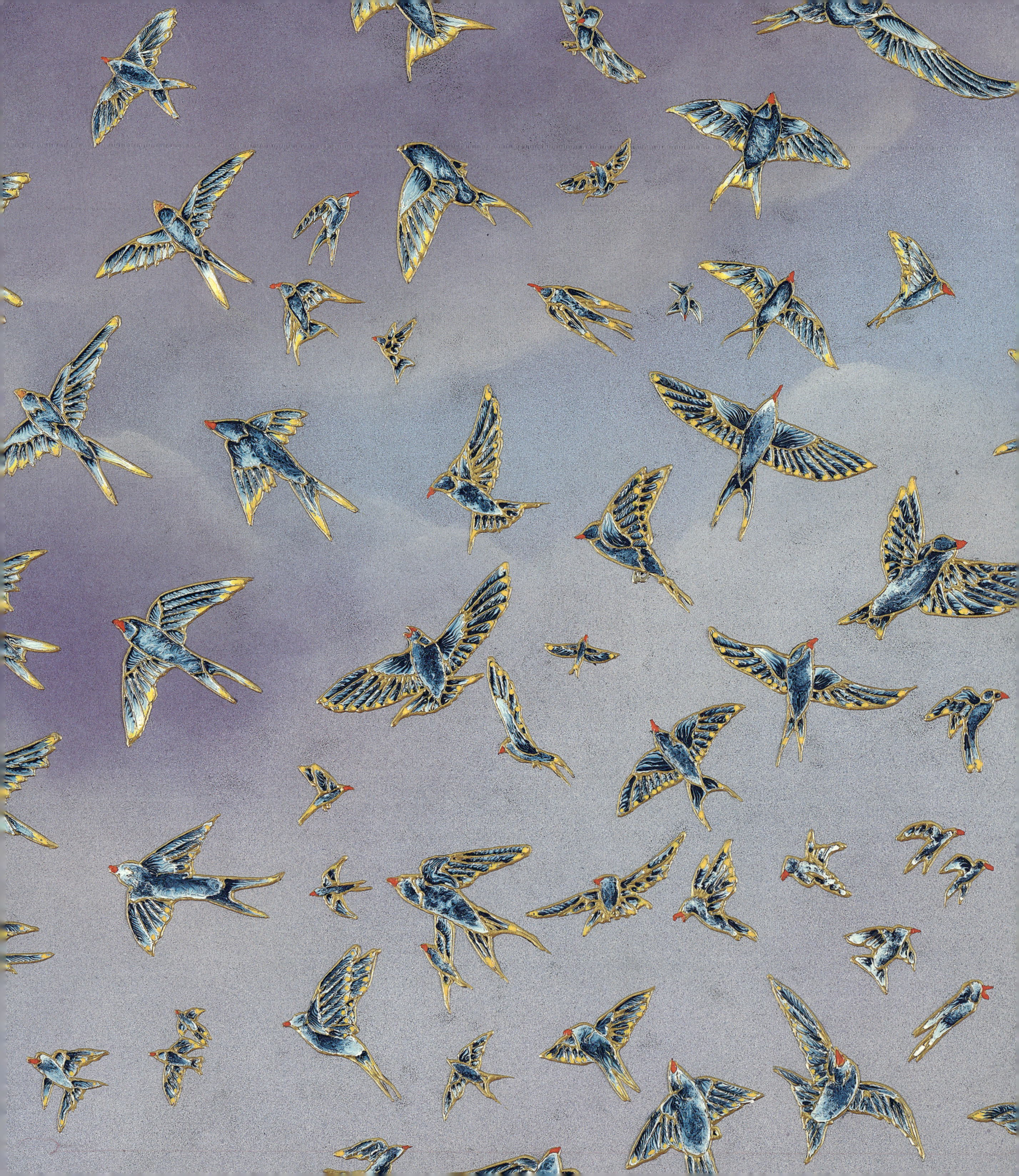